The Heart of the World

by Ned Rozell

As long as I live, I'll hear waterfalls and birds and winds sing.

*I'll interpret the rocks, learn the language of
flood, storm, and avalanche.*

I'll acquaint myself with the glaciers and wild gardens,

and get as near the heart of the world as I can.

John Muir, 1871

CONTENTS

Fairbanks
(Chena Marina Airstrip)
to
Black Rapids Glacier
~120 air miles

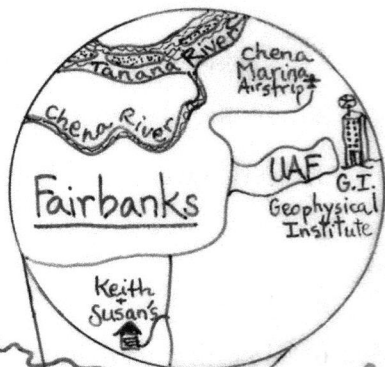

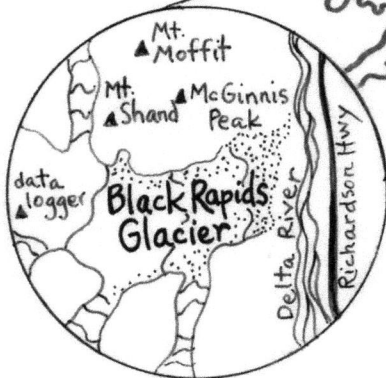

N

Fairbanks

Tanana River
Chena River
Chena Marina Airstrip
UAF
G.I.
Geophysical Institute
Keith + Susan's

Alaska
Brooks Range
Arctic Circle
Russia
Fairbanks
Alaska Range
Anchorage
Canada
Juneau

Mt. Moffit
Mt. Shand
McGinnis Peak
data logger
Black Rapids Glacier
Delta River
Richardson Hwy

1 | A sign

The center of Alaska, early May. The cluck of wood frogs in chilly pools of snowmelt, their bodies squishy after months frozen hard as rocks. Up in the sprucetops, the big songs of thumb-size kinglets newly arrived from Costa Rica. Swollen buds at the end of branches unrolling into balsam poplar leaves, sticky and smelling like mint. Billions of solar panels reaching for a sun shining down for an additional hour each week. Those who remembered the midnight black of December afternoons prepared to cram a year of outdoor activity into three brilliant months.

Tall, shaggy-haired with a full moustache and dimpled chin, Keith Echelmeyer had plans for the season of light. In rubber boots and with a bouncy stride, he approached his airplane, a single-engine Piper PA-12.

Built just after World War II, the PA-12, FAA approved for wheels, skis, floats and crop spraying, might have been designed for bush Alaska.

In 1947, two pilots flew a pair of PA-12s around the world. Their worst mechanical problem was a cracked tailwheel. In the years since, many of the nimble craft (lighter than a half-ton pickup) have found their way north to Alaska, a state with 736 airports. Most are surfaced with local gravel, but the tail-dragger (with a wheel under its back end) can land on the river-sorted rocks of wilderness floodplains.

With the May sun rising before 5 and setting after 11, the aurora borealis was a memory in interior Alaska. The daylight and the energy it transferred had people up at 10 p.m. tilling gardens and framing houses. Even in the time of infinite illumination they could sense Alaska's longest season, hunched on the other side of August.

Today was another day of as many flights as Echelmeyer could manage. His repeated round trips were from an airstrip near the mid-size city of Fairbanks over unpeopled country to a strip 150 miles south. There, next to Alaska Route 4, was a wide expanse of windy gray river and a glacier that made it swell, Black Rapids.

Black Rapids was the most dramatic landlocked glacier in Alaska. In 1936, Black Rapids appeared in Time magazine after people reported it moving toward an Alaska highway at more than 200 feet each day. Its advance was an oddity, as most Alaska glaciers were fading into the mountains.

For reasons unknown, Black Rapids suddenly stopped and reversed course. The Galloping Glacier has shrunk ever since. But its past behavior had attracted scientists like Echelmeyer. Scientists chose "surging" to describe Black Rapids and just a dozen of Alaska's other 100,000 glaciers. Those mavericks for some reason get up and go, after decades of hardly moving at all. Why?

In 2002, long after the glacier had withdrawn from view of highway drivers, Echelmeyer needed to answer that question. With unlimited choices of what to study, he chose a discipline that combined cold mountains with the equation-rich physics of ice. He studied glaciers in Antarctica, Patagonia, Greenland, Washington. He had a knack for being able to find the quirk, the characteristic that made an ice body unique.

He designed a long-term study on Black Rapids that National Science Foundation officials funded even though at the time they favored research on the big ice sheets of Antarctica and Greenland.

His study engaged half a dozen graduate students, a few technicians and a mechanic. On the ice, midway up the glacier, he had transported a snowmobile, a diesel hot water drill and a half-mile of hose to penetrate to the base of the glacier. Tents and skis and food and people. Flight after flight.

Echelmeyer loved Black Rapids because it was pretty much his. It was far enough from any town that few people went there to ski or climb, in summer a raging river blocked access and pilots didn't land there often.

He savored the flights that got him there. When heavy with equipment, he'd turn up the Wood River and punch through a low pass in airspace that was all his. His wheel-skis — hybrid landing gear with tires protruding from what look like water skis — allowed landings either on snow or gravel. Less than two hours after lifting off packed rocks in Fairbanks he would slide on the glacier.

When he did not fly directly to the glacier, such as during

his May shuttles of people and gear for the big study, Echelmeyer landed at the airstrip that paralleled the Richardson Highway. There, he often removed items from the plane and left them in the grass by the airstrip. He needed to be lighter for the jump across the river and uphill landing on last winter's snow.

Sometimes, using a stepladder and five-gallon jugs, he refueled the Piper at the Black Rapids strip. Whenever he stopped moving, his mind returned to The List.

First, there were the things that needed to be flown to the upper third of Black Rapids: The engine for the hot-water driller, the hoses, the tiltmeters that would detect the glacier's movement. The people, who had driven down from Fairbanks and parked their trucks in the willows by the airstrip. Their duffels and dry bags and coolers.

Then there was the paper he had almost finished. Echelmeyer, regarded by his peers as a genius in physics and theoretical math, had written or coauthored a few dozen journal articles on glacier ice. This one was different. It was the culmination of hundreds of his repeated flights along the length of Alaska and Pacific Northwest glaciers. Using a laser rangefinding system mounted in the belly of his plane, he had measured the precise height of those 67 glaciers, year after year.

His field-hand technicians did the number crunching for him. They subtracted the glacier heights from Echelmeyer's decade-plus of flights from the elevations of white glacial ice on topographic maps drawn in the 1950s. Much of the ice had shrunk the height of the tallest buildings in Fairbanks.

He found that Alaska glaciers, though tiny in area compared to Greenland, were dumping almost twice as much fresh water into the oceans. It was an absurd notion that glaciers scattered in one mountainous region could match the giant ice cap. Though Alaska glaciers made up only 13 percent of the planet's glacier ice, they were causing 50 percent of worldwide glacial contribution to sea-level rise.

Echelmeyer was a scientist, not an alarmist. But the ice was telling a story few had imagined.

This was too big for the Journal of Glaciology. He aimed for the top, sending it to the editors at Science, the bible of scientific legitimacy. The editors accepted the paper, with some revisions for style.

Inserting the changes kept him up until reluctant stars poked through the dusky night. In his home in the birch forest off Eldorado Drive, with his wife Susan Campbell asleep downstairs, he would turn on the desk lamp and think about how to fix the red marks on the text. He pushed past his urge to sleep, knowing that this document, at what he guessed was the midpoint of his career, would be read more than anything he had written.

As if the paper and the field campaign on Black Rapids weren't enough, there were the physics classes he was teaching. He had to write new questions for a final exam, which he'd be giving in a few days, and grading after that.

Then there were the countless last-minute details to be wrapped up before the conference in Yakutat he was organizing. It's difficult to put on a large gathering in a city. He had chosen a fishing village of 640 surrounded by glaciers, reachable only by boat or plane. The conference was one month away.

As the red plastic five-gallon jug sucked air and flooded gas into the Piper's wing tank, Echelmeyer squeezed the molded handle with his right hand. His forearm tensed. He felt strong, able to hold the 40 pounds of liquid at arm's length.

Not like yesterday, when he'd dropped a wrench while twisting a propane connection. Such moments were occurring often enough to have been added to The List. Those times at the computer when his hand went numb. Or when he was flying and needed to look down and make sure he was still grasping the floor stick that is the main controller of the PA-12.

He thought it might be carpal tunnel syndrome, a common enough affliction for those who spent hours hunched at a desk. The loss of feeling in his right hand worried him enough that he visited a doctor in Fairbanks who specialized in joint and bone disorders. Something was going on, the doctor agreed, but he didn't think it was carpal tunnel.

One night, after a day of three-round trip flights to Black Rapids, he once again noticed a lack of sensation as he drove the unpaved road home to Susan. His right hand gripped the steering wheel, but he could not feel it.

Susan, having finished preparing her third-grade class lessons for the next day, had baked salmon over rice.

They held hands across the table and gave thanks for the fish. He couldn't feel her warmth through his right fingers.

"What if it's something really bad?" he said.

"That's ridiculous. You're doing all this flying and writing all those proposals and papers," Susan said. "It's just all this stress."

"Yeah, but what if it's something else?"

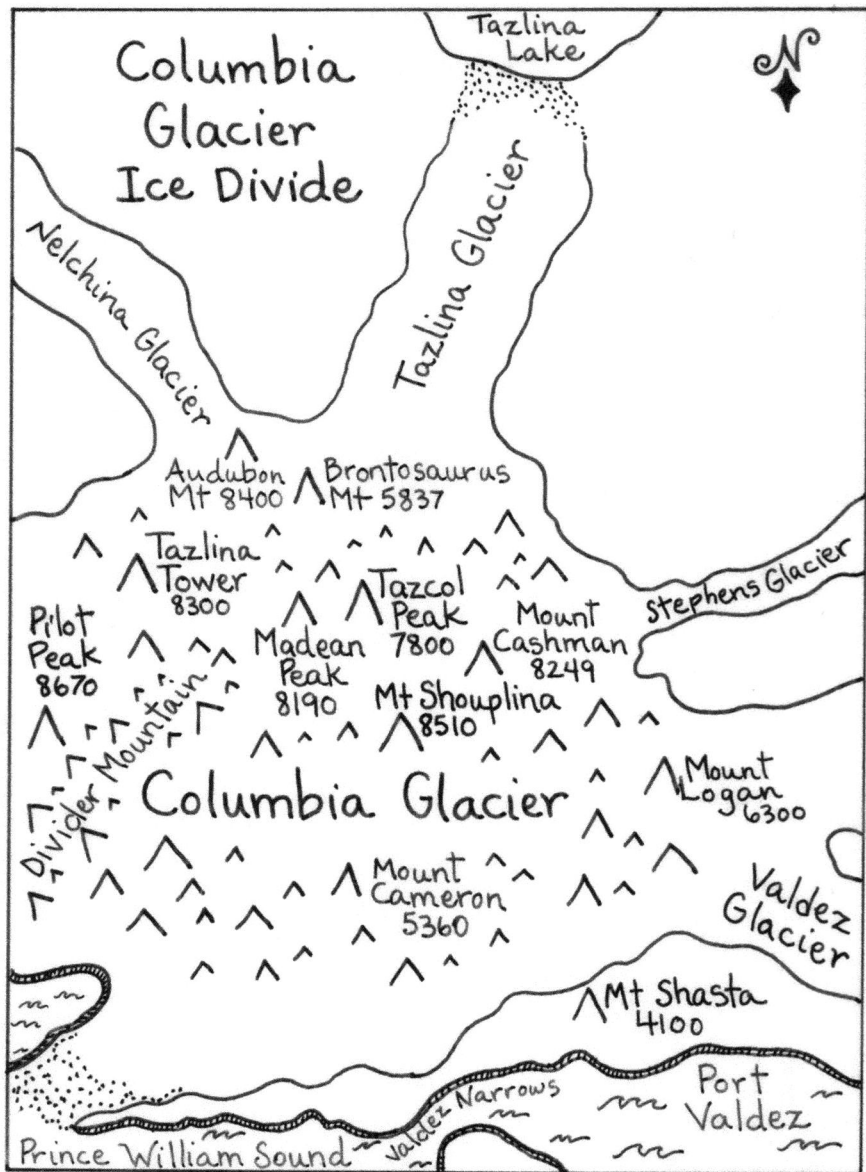

Columbia
Glacier
Ice Divide

Tazlina
Lake

Nelchina Glacier

Tazlina Glacier

Stephens Glacier

Audubon
Mt 8400

Brontosaurus
Mt 5837

Tazlina
Tower
8300

Tazcol
Peak
7800

Mount
Cashman
8249

Pilot
Peak
8670

Madean
Peak
8190

Mt Shouplina
8510

Divider Mountain

Columbia Glacier

Mount
Logan
6300

Mount
Cameron
5360

Valdez
Glacier

Mt Shasta
4100

Port
Valdez

Valdez Narrows

Prince William Sound

2 | Flying glaciers

The Chugach Mountains are castle walls that protect interior Alaska from moisture sheeting inland from the Gulf of Alaska. At the crown of the range, about 10,000 feet above the ocean, snow falls in feet, not inches.

There perches an icefield pierced by mountaintops too steep to hold snow. From the divide, fingers of ice reach inland to the warm, dry heart of Alaska and south, toward the mist of Prince William Sound.

No one lives where the ice is, but an old timer driving to his boat in Valdez watched Worthington Glacier retreat from the highway for 40 years. He could almost touch the blue face back then. Now, it's a 15-minute hike to the ice over clean, round gravel.

Only three glaciers in Alaska had anyone measuring them a long time. That trio — one in the Alaska Range and two on the coast — are all fading faster than snows are replenishing them. What about the other hundred thousand?

Will Harrison, the tall, blunt lead of the glacier lab, could see the future as his unshowered colleague bounced into the office.

"Look at this," Harrison said, slapping a printed NASA proposal on Echelmeyer's desk. "Millions to fly a twin-engine jet over icefields. Reflecting a laser off the ice to get the elevation.

"We should put one of these in the PA-12. You could fly all the mountain glaciers in Alaska. We could get a handle on what's happening all over the state. And we can beat the hell out of that price."

Here was a potential task that would feed Echelmeyer in many ways.

He read the NASA proposal about installing a laser on the underside of a jet that flew at high altitude over ice sheets. The laser would strike the whitish surface, leaving an invisible trail along its length. The beam reflected back to a sensor on the plane. A computer onboard would use GPS and other signals to calculate the precise height of the ice sheets. In this way, glaciologists could later compare the elevations in order to determine how much had the ice shrunk or risen since the last flight.

It was a timely idea, one that covered more ground than strapping on crampons and measuring the movement of stakes driven into the glacier the year before. USGS glaciologists had done these measures for years on the three Alaska glaciers.

The new idea: Fly over the deck of these small mountain glaciers, close enough to see a raven walking the ice. Get a precision measurement. Compare the Piper's elevations with the ones USGS mapmakers drew on the topos in 1940s and 50s.

That idea led here: Rattling along 150 feet above Tazlina Glacier, Virginia Valentine in the back, her Ziploc within reach in case she had to puke.

"Now," Echelmeyer said.

Better known as By, Virginia Valentine tapped three letters on the keyboard resting on her lap. At her back was the tower brain of a computer, behind that a box with a laser aimed downward through a hole in the Piper.

"Profiling," By said.

Echelmeyer flew dead north, down Tazlina's 25 miles of ice. The laser sent light pulses to the ice. They bounced back to the plane. An instrument onboard calculated the time it took for the light to return. That simple time delay, after many athletic calculations by Dan, Anthony, Sandy, By, Chris and others, equaled the precise elevation of the glacier. This was the gold amid mountains of gravel.

"Terminus," Echelmeyer said over the headset mic. He referred to the end of the glacier, where the gray ice turned to dirty boulders. From the snout, a cold brownish flow splashed through the rocks into Tazlina Lake, a watery impression of the glacier, almost as long.

By hit a few keys to stop the profiling as Echelmeyer flew over Tazlina Lake. He banked hard for a U-turn. By tasted salt water behind her tongue. She reached for her bag. But he leveled the Piper and aimed straight and smooth.

He aimed for the ice divide between Tazlina, whose meltwater flowed to the Copper River, and Columbia Glacier, which direct-deposits to Prince William Sound. Columbia is one of the most dynamic, visible glaciers in Alaska, calving its bergs into Prince William Sound. Oil-tanker captains sailing their behemoths from Valdez to refineries in California throttle down on occasion to bump Columbia's ice out of their way.

"We'll land here by Brontosaurus Mountain," Echelmeyer said, pointing to a five-mile tabletop of ice and snow that fed both Tazlina and Columbia.

By braced for the friction of skis on snow as Echelmeyer touched down in the palm of the pass. From there spilled a dozen glaciers, among them the collegiate Harvard and Yale, named along with Columbia by members of the Harriman Expedition in 1899.

After the PA-12 stopped sliding, Echelmeyer unbuckled and creaked his door open. He cupped By's elbow and helped her to the ice. From the cramped cab, it was like stepping on the moon. She gulped fresh, clean air that carried a wisp of hot metal. The engine ticked as it cooled.

Echelmeyer screwed together the copper rods that made up a snow probe. Knowing she had a few moments before she had to scribble with pad and pencil, By rotated herself in slow motion. Her hiking boots made a circular imprint on the snow as she drank in the view.

She was in a world she never imagined. A South Carolina girl who migrated north, By got the job with Keith because she was adept at complex things, like turning all these measurements into a number that represented glacial change. Here, she was in a white hush, standing at the same elevation as Denver. Winter storms, ancient and modern, deposited uncountable snow grains there. Distance from the equator and long cold winters had allowed it to endure.

By flashed back to a year before, when Echelmeyer first deposited her on Black Rapids Glacier. She was new to the glaciers lab then. Echelmeyer assigned her to wear a GPS in a backpack; he trusted her, expected her to ski to another point on the glacier. She would act as a human version of the profiling aircraft, to ground-truth the instruments.

Her first reaction: *can I do this?* Her second emotion, as Echelmeyer roared off for the upper lobe of Black Rapids and silence wrapped her like an embryo. *I've never been this far from a road before.*

There in the Chugach, as she watched Echelmeyer twist the copper rod, another memory. It was again Black Rapids, 30 below. He hadn't planned to be there at such a temperature. But things change. She and Patty Delvecchio, who flew many profiles with Echelmeyer, watched as he screwed the sections together with bare hands, because the job was impossible with gloves. They both had the same thought. Cold doesn't affect him.

The temperature on that trip to Black Rapids had also dropped beneath the operating specifications of the Piper PA-12. Its engine oil had hardened as it cooled, trapping the pistons like insects in amber. With bare fingers Echelmeyer assembled his MSR camping stove, fired it and snaked aluminum ductwork from the stove to a hole in the cowling over his engine. In an hour the oil would be warm, allowing Echelmeyer to start the engine. Glaciologist Chris Larson said Echelmeyer could will himself not to be cold. *He's Luke Skywalker. Keith has the force.*

On the Tazlina/Columbia ice divide, she watched Echelmeyer shoving the copper rod through the snow surface. Will said the instrument started life as a tank antenna. It was one of Echelmeyer's go-to measuring devices; he had pushed it to hard ice hundreds of times, always keeping an eye on the sky for a weather change. And scanning nearby grades to see if they might be skiable.

Virginia Valentine admired her boss for his abilities to make the semi-impossible happen on a regular basis, to know and defy the forces he worked against. Climbing mountains, solving the trickiest physics problems, showing up for class the day after a month-long expedition and belting out a good lecture. *I wonder what he thinks of us mere mortals?*

She admired, but did not envy him. The pressure he faced every day. The stress he transferred to his charges, none of whom shared the breadth of his talents. And the boilover points. When he shouted at Patty after she returned from the library with that book on GIS. *I don't want you to learn how to do it. I just want you to do it!*

He was the star player turned manager. The guy who couldn't understand why his first baseman couldn't hit the curveball. See it, hit it. What's so hard?

Despite the days spent together in sublime places, By never felt a connection to Echelmeyer. He wasn't an easy conversation, like Will was. He didn't seem to have the time or interest to ponder the lives of his grad students and the hired hands like herself. To her, he was driven and opaque. Pleasant much of the time, but inaccessible. He was a person she would invite to her college graduation but not her birthday party.

"Three meters, 27 centimeters," Echelmeyer said. By scribbled the depth of the new snow in her yellow notebook, happy for the spring sun that warmed her black liner gloves.

"Let's get a few profiles on Columbia," Echelmeyer said. "We've got enough light for the east branch and second branch. Should be back in Valdez for dinner."

And they were. There are degrees of difficulty to flying a small plane. Flying in gaps between mountains above chilled bodies of ice requires uncommon skills and awareness. A pilot must not only react to sudden wind and weather changes, but anticipate them. And there are few places a pilot could look for more sudden weather changes than the swirls and shears above glaciers and the ridges that wall them in. Each takeoff and landing a frantic masterpiece.

Echelmeyer's icy empire. He flew Tazlina, Gulkana, Toklat, Susitna, Tustumena, Turquoise, Columbia, Malaspina, McCall. Dozens of others. Flight after flight. Brooks Range, Chugach Mountains, Wrangells, Alaska Range. Even the few glaciers tucked in the Kuskokwim Mountains near Bristol Bay.

The odometer mileage during the time the laser was turned on equaled the distance from Fairbanks to South Africa, all flown in a single-engine aircraft. Yanked by the wind, snotty weather, emergency landings and takeoffs delayed by the need to stomp out a ramp in the snow. Objective risk.

Why do it? Because scientists obsessed with big ice sheets

were underestimating what Echelmeyer and others called mountain glaciers. And because it was fun.

Mount Hayes

E

hanging ice
accretions

← 80 miles
Fairbanks

Richardson Hwy.

North Ridge

bivoac

NW
Face

Trident
Glacier

wolf
tracks

cub landing
spot

bergshrund
camp

Hayes Glacier

crevasses

ice chunk
field

18

3 | Northwest face, Mount Hayes

If, on a certain spring evening, Will Harrison had pointed a telescope out his 6th floor window at the Geophysical Institute and looked southward, he would have seen what looked like two spiders, hanging by strings from a triangular white peak.

If Harrison had realized those spiders were his protégé Keith and Keith's friend Jon Miller, suspended in mid-air while halted on an attempt to knock off the northwest face of Mount Hayes, he would have laughed his ass off.

The attempt at a mountaineering line not yet accomplished had started well for Keith and his good friend.

When Keith, still fastened to his skis after the approach from the Richardson Highway, squinted upward from the ice of Trident Glacier, an ashen bulge one mile up on Mount Hayes promised comfort.

It seemed to be a cling of cold rock, with maybe enough level space for he and Jon to rest during the climb. Perhaps it would offer a break from the incessant exposure to stones and ice tumbling down the polished, blue-gray ice face.

Hours later, at headlamp time, Keith and Jon came to a

sad realization. Their hoped-for bivouac site was a wall of crumbling schist. There was no surface resembling flat, and no amount of work would make it that way.

Jon, who was leading the climb and was sticking to the mountain by the points of his crampons and the tip of his ice axe, had to figure out what to do next.

He twisted an ice screw — a steel anchor that can hold a man's weight — into the mountain wall. He clipped a carabiner through a screw eye, then tied his rope in with a clove hitch. It was his connection to Mount Hayes for the night.

Jon turned a second ice screw into the wall an arm's length from the first. One each for his and Keith's bodies, but with a backup nylon sling running between them, in case one of them failed.

Surveying the scene and the few objects in his possession, Jon decided to try something he never had — use his pack as a bag in which to insert both feet, in order to take some of his weight off his harness.

Why stand in your backpack? Because Keith and Jon had been wrong; that bulge in the mountain they had seen from below was not a good resting spot. It offered as much comfort as the skin of a skyscraper.

With darkness coming and exhaustion already heavy within both of them, they had to create the best shelter they could. With the aid of their packs, they prepped to spend the night hanging from the northwest face of Mount Hayes.

There, Jon and Keith felt the cold of March, which promises

heat but is slow to deliver. With measured haste, they needed to execute a few delicate maneuvers before they could rest. For one thing, they needed to get at their sleeping bags, buried within their packs.

First though, everything had to be secured to the ice wall, to be hung from the two ice screws.

Jon shed his pack and clicked the two shoulder straps into carabiners. Hanging from the rope tied to his waist harness by a figure 8 knot, he kicked his crampons off his boots with care and difficulty.

Without crampons — steel toe-points jabbing the ice like picks — there was zero purchase. All his weight was on the rope.

With crampons off, he pulled his sleeping bag from his pack, being careful never to let it go. If he dropped it, or anything else, that object would fall 4,000 feet to their starting point, the ice of Trident Glacier.

Jon then wriggled into his sleeping bag, pulling it over his harness and around the rope as best he could. He wormed his legs into the mouth of his backpack.

The pack received his 145 pounds, nylon straining to transfer the stress to his ice screw. It held. The pack took much of Jon's weight off his climbing harness, allowing his knees, feet and butt to take some of his weight.

He was a lumpy caterpillar oozing out of a chrysalis on the side of a white mountain.

"It's warm!" Jon said. He smiled at Keith, who had duplicated Jon's careful movements.

Keith scrunched into his trusty blue pack, inside the red sleeping bag rated for zero but aged to 20 above. The heat came to his legs and then his torso, but not like the delicious first step into a sauna. It was more like waiting for the car heater at 30 below.

Hanging in backpacks was not what either man wanted to do, but it was their best option to pass the dark hours. They could not proceed up a mountain they could not see.

Next came the chore of making water to drink, made much harder by their location.

Into the wall, Jon swung the ax, gently. Ice shattered and cracks ran. Both men stopped breathing, hoping the fracture would not compromise the solidity of the two screws from which their worlds were hanging.

Keith chipped an ice shelf for the stove. He clipped both the stove bottle and the pot into the pink sling.

Jon skittered ice chips into the pot. In half an hour, he melted enough water to fill two mugs.

A breeze stole their body heat. Their heads nodded, then jerked awake. Sleep seemed more pressing than water, but they knew it was not. Water warmed them, cleared their heads.

The friends could see, in the distant twilight, the shimmering lights of Fairbanks. Within the pulsating yellow of the city core were car dealerships and box stores. Those on the evening shifts were getting ready to punch out, and step into cars warmed by autostart.

The view of tungsten lights was an unexpected connection to that other world, the one in which 100,000 humans were surrounded by millions of acres of blackness. Within the flicker, all that stuff by which people define themselves — big houses burning heating oil, offices with nameplates on the door and tenure-review paperwork on the desk.

And, Will Harrison might be up there in his office, peering out a scope and laughing.

Keith turned his head and saw Jon, sipping cocoa from his mug.

Jon was a California boy. Keith met him two years before. He knew a few things about Jon: he studied rosy finches, had smiling eyes and was a carpenter.

Jon appreciated things besides the line he was climbing. He puzzled over the age of curling wolverine tracks in blue snow. He knew when to back off, and was a governor for alpine overoptimism. He was a good technical problem solver, with a huge capacity for suffering in silence. Most important to Keith, Jon was trustworthy.

And they were experiencing one of those times you need to believe in a friend: 4,000 feet up the 6,000-foot northwesterly wall of Hayes. In spring, the pyramid turned orange sherbet from Keith's (and Will's) office windows. The mountain was 80 miles from town on the wings of a raven.

Their climb to the wall had gone like this: They reached

their perch by moving fast — one screw for every 300 feet of rope lead, what climbers call psychological protection.

They swung leads at first, then, when the sun slanted low, they took advantage of their differing strengths. Jon, with insect power-to-weight ratio but no bulk, handed Keith 15 pounds of gear. In exchange, Jon led every pitch nimbly and quickly: placing a screw, belaying, ticking off again.

Whock. Whock. Click. Click. The men's existence rang out in a four-part tempo. Ice ax in their left hand, north wall hammer (pick on one end, blunt iron on the other) in their dominant right. They aimed for depressions, rough patches, pre-existing cracks to help their picks penetrate, and to ease the jarring. Stepping up, swinging their boot — heel low for maximum front point bite.

It was too much work to get a perfect placement every time, so the climbers made sure of two anchor points — even better, three — for those infrequent, inevitable times when a clinging tool popped, or a shift of weight shattered the ice around crampon points.

On the way up, the blow of Jon's ice tool sent a crack echoing across the face, redistributing its internal stresses.

Jon yelled.

"Ice!"

On every ice climb, pieces fall. Mostly shards, but this time a dinner plate flew toward Keith on the rope below. Three-hundred feet of acceleration, the disc whistled down the slope.

The ice bit Keith's left arm. With a changed trajectory as it deflected off him, the ice fell to Trident Glacier.

"Fuck!" Keith yelled. "Crab, you asshole!"

Bill Echelmeyer, Keith's Dad, flashed on Keith's mindscreen: I'll meet you at the top. Bill Echelmeyer once left a whiny eight-year old on the trail to get over himself. Sobbing, alone for an hour, until there his dad was, sitting on a rock, squinting at the plain of eastern Colorado. Keith didn't get a hug when he finally caught up. You can eat your sandwich now.

I got a lot of things from him, Keith thought on the mountainside. Always, it's two tigers fighting; the bitter, pissed one and the appreciative, loving one. Which one wins? He had been learning that answer for years. The one that's fed.

Keith wondered: Did Jon even hear me call him an asshole? But Jon reacted by skittering sideways on the wall, so the debris line was not directly above Keith.

Later, there cramped in his backpack, Keith didn't apologize to Jon. But he did try to appreciate where they were, a place two humans had surely never dangled.

Keith pulled his wool hat down and secured it on his brow and buried his hands in his crotch. His breath turned everything clean and white. His legs tingled, going numb even with the weight off the harness. There were seven hours left to dangle, until the sun would rise again.

There in the darkness, the fang of Mount Hayes was first to feel the weather change. It started small, as a breeze that announced itself with a whisper. Then it shoved the packs, inducing a slight rocking that was not soothing.

The lights of Fairbanks smeared, like a watercolor left in the rain. Then blackness. The tightest squint could not bring those lights back. Town was gone. There was the mountain and Jon and the webbing and tools and the whir of the wind.

Midnight, Keith's watch said. Life inside a lenticular cloud began. With the first gusts, spindrift poured down the mountain face and sintered into every crack.

Keith reached for the clipped-in tent fabric. He and Jon wound it around the dual packs, like a beach towel wrapped around twins. Their mouths pressed to openings to breathe fresh, snowy air. The little thermometer, which didn't get to taste wind, said five below.

Keith woke with a start. Dawn. Finally.

He was still there, hanging. It was snowing, hard. Avalanche joined the list of what might make this their ultimate trip. They blinked the frost off their eyelashes. Their legs were logs folded in backpacks, wrapped by tent nylon, covered in white powder.

Jon was first to try his mouth.

"Descent," steam curled from his lips. "Rappel."

"Down? Are you sure?" Keith said. "The top's a lot closer."

Both heard his waver, his bluff. And there was no queue of climbers below on Hayes Glacier waiting to try the first winter ascent. The northwest face would be there another day.

"OK. Down," Keith said.

On their descent, Keith and Jon heard a roar that speaks only in the mountains. Avalanche!

They braced for contact, and prayed for spindrift. Spindrift it was, hissing and splashing around them. Snow crystals penetrated every fiber, defeating Gore Tex, stinking polypro and wool, melting against their skin.

Keith forced a smile, realizing that they were not swept off the face. But the ice physicist knew it was then snowing and blowing so hard that hardened slabs were building above them. If they got heavy enough to release, Keith and Jon's thin rope would not save them.

But the grains sluffed; they were cohesionless masses that knocked snow from their paths, like sighs of relief. After a dozen showers of snow crystals, Keith and Jon ignored the whoosh. They knew the bits of snow were like tiny earthquakes releasing the stress on a fault.

Energized, they thought of nothing but focus. They rappelled, rappelled, rappelled. More than 20 of these jumps back off the face, to descend in a hurry.

First, they used the hardware-store electrical conduit, pounded into ice screw holes as cheap anchors to clip the rope into. When a rock appeared, they drove metal pitons as the link to the mountain.

Most of that hardware is still stuck in Mount Hayes, left behind for speed and safety. Keith hated that part. He was the guy who couldn't leave a fire ring without throwing the charred sticks into the woods and sweeping dirt with a spruce bough. It was his spiritual bequeathal to the next person. But sometimes there was no choice.

One more rappel. They no longer felt the boyish thrill of flying off the wall like Spiderman. They winced and sprung backward.

After one last leap, their leaden feet hit the clear blue surface of Trident Glacier.

After 20 hours of descent, their femurs loaded and feeling strange, they swayed on new legs. Jon unclipped his carabiner, fell to the ice and panted.

They staggered to a camp within a bergshrund, a mini-crevasse that yawned protection from the wind. Keith set up the tent. Both men lurched inside and pulled their sleeping bags over their legs. Keith fired the camp stove.

They sipped their first water since when they were dangling, in almost one day of maximum effort. Hot water warmed their chests. Jon smiled. Both men were drowsily ecstatic, destroyed with release.

After 10 hours, during which the ice of the glacier hummed with dueling snores from a Bibler tent, they packed up.

They began a meditative ski out to the highway. There was a bliss in not hanging, in their skis polishing the snow with free movement.

"Stop," Jon said.

Their skis and plastic sleds halted, as did the ponderous

noise they created. Keith and Jon listened to the static of silence.

Yes — they both heard it. A howl.

A few more wolves joined in. It pierced their souls, a different penetration than the aura of the mountain.

If there was one creature both of them identified with, it was this one. Wiped out in Colorado and most everywhere else. Yet there they were, sniffing the air, noses wrinkling at bitter human.

The wolves turned at the scent and moved, gray ghosts flowing over Trident Glacier. And then they were gone.

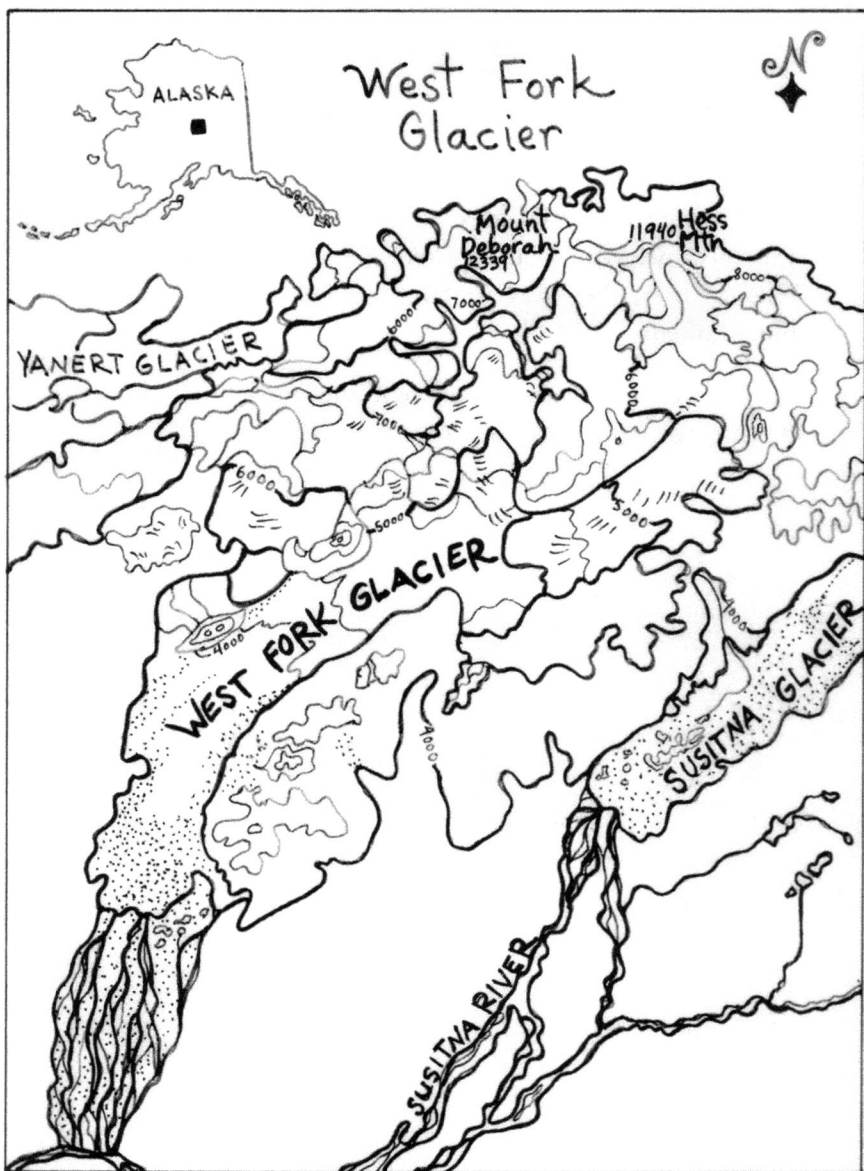

West Fork
Glacier

ALASKA

N

Mount
Deborah
12339

11940 Hess
Mtn

8000

7000

6000

YANERT GLACIER

4000

6000

6000

5000

5000

WEST FORK GLACIER

4000

4000

4000

SUSITNA GLACIER

SUSITNA RIVER

4 | Throwing spruce

Keith shoved open the door of the PA-12. Cold wind knifed into the eyes of Gary Holton in the back seat. Holton blinked away tears. Then he wrapped his glove around the prickly stem of a four-foot spruce tree.

"Throw it hard, so it doesn't hit the tail," Keith yelled.

Holton couldn't suppress a chuckle. Until a few minutes ago, he did not know throwing trees from planes was part of the script.

"OK. Now!"

Holton grunted as he pushed the spruce. The sky sucked it out like a vacuum. Loose needles tickled their cheeks. The tree wafted to the fractured surface of the West Fork Glacier. It landed with a whoosh no one heard.

Keith slammed the door and latched it.

"Good," he said over the headset.

Holton nodded even though Keith couldn't see him. Somewhat new to Alaska, Holton was a mathematician Keith recruited to help apply numerical models to the flow of glacier ice. The models could, in theory, fill data holes, to tell a glaciologist more about how a valley glacier flowed.

Like everyone else who worked with Keith, Holton became a field Sherpa. He was tough, wiry, up for adventure.

A few hours and four trees into the day on West Fork Glacier, after landing on the glacier in the afternoon, Keith swiveled a camera box to point at a distant tree perched on a crevasse field. In the hiss of mountain silence, Holton, seated on a gray rock, had a question.

"So, what would happen if a tree hit the tail?"

"Oh, it wouldn't be good."

Another time, flying in the Brooks Range, Keith turned to him.

"Can you take the stick? I want to take some pictures of this wall. I'd like to climb it later."

Holton grabbed the control stick between his legs, the one slaved to Keith's in front. He was then flying the plane, trying to maintain course. The stick seemed so sensitive; the plane veered when he thought about moving. The Piper drifted closer to the mountain. Keith, eyes not lifting from the camera viewfinder, gave instructions.

"Press harder with your foot on the right rudder pedal," he said. "That will keep us away."

The plane responded as Holton strained his right quad. Keith got his shot.

"OK, I've got her now," he said.

Keith took over and peeled off, back toward Fairbanks.

Other field assistants had said enough. Some said the possibility of crashing was too high, even if Keith was learning from each expensive mistake. Another small group, of which Holton was still a member, thought walking on icefields that had felt the tread of few boots outweighed the risk.

Keith was like a little boy: Spotting climbers on Mount Hayes and zooming over so he could wag wings at friends clinging to the ice. Grinning as he grunted a 100-pound pack to his shoulders, schlepping gear into Fels Glacier from the highway.

Holton heard some of these tales while sharing a tent on Jacobshavn in Greenland. There, he helped Keith shove a hotwater drill into the glacier, an act that enabled the discovery that the world's fastest glacier was moving even quicker than anyone thought.

Holton, now a linguist and former mathematician, saw Keith's creativity every day in the field. The hot water drilling in Greenland was a unique plan to get to the bottom of a glacier (though it did not work there, it did other places). The use of mathematical models to understand glacier movement was then novel. And a Christmas tree thrown to the surface of a glacier made for a low-cost visual marker that was also biodegradable.

But when Keith swooped down to check out bison on the floodplain of the Delta River, or when he pulled out his pee bottle and asked his passenger to fly the plane, Holton wondered to himself if perhaps things should be the other way around. *He* should be the pilot. A person with Keith's curiosity could then squint out the window and report that the grizzly was squirting blueberries from its rear as it ran.

Keith appreciated Gary Holton because he was one of very few who could talk theoretical math and understand how that applied to a river of ice. Holton seemed to also like camping in cold, quiet places and did not seem to complain with methods used to get the work done.

Like tossing trees from an airplane. The fallen spruce was to be photographed by a time-lapse camera, to see how the glacier moved over time. The 35-millimeter film cameras were housed in a plastic box. They took one photograph each day when they were working. Often, they were not, sometimes when a bear swatted the box off a tripod, or batteries failed, or the wispy spruce disappeared from the camera's field of view.

As that February light ripened to orange on that tree-dropping trip, Keith thought of another camera overlooking the West Fork. They probably had time to swap out a roll of film before the hour flight back to Fairbanks. It would save gas later.

"Let's check on WF7 before we head back," he said.

The landing spot was a snow bench above the middle portion of the West Fork Glacier, which flowed from the central Alaska Range almost to the gravel of the Denali Highway. With Holton aboard, Keith had landed there a few weeks earlier. The ski tracks of the Piper were still visible, but soft. As hard as

Keith squinted, he could not sharpen them.

Keith circled the Piper and came in straight. It was like the half dozen landings he had made earlier in the day, except for the deteriorating light. His tracks no longer jumped at him.

Holton held his breath as the Piper glided in for the landing.

Three seconds before impact, both men saw, suddenly in sharp focus, a mound of snow almost close enough to touch.

"Shit!"

With a meaty thud and the ping of sheared aluminum, the plane smacked into the slope. The Piper slid three plane lengths on the snow until the broken ski mounts bit and the plane jerked to a halt.

They had come in short, a few hundred feet downslope of the old tracks. Holton remembers a blow to the chin delivered from the back of the pilot's seat. His seatbelt was unbuckled, the better to throw trees.

Keith had thrust forward, the harness burning a V into his shoulders. When he bounced back, he reached forward and killed the engine. The mountain went silent.

"Jesus, are you OK?" Keith said.

"I think so," Holton said, hand squeezing his chin.

Their situation: Shaken up, but no broken bones or disabling injuries. The front landing gear — the pair of skis installed where wheels would be in summer — was crunched and unusable. A bent strut. Possibly a dinged propeller. The plane was unflyable.

As reddish light bathed the hillside, the two men climbed out of the PA-12, which lay flat on its belly. The smell of gasoline stung their nostrils.

Keith didn't lament the situation, or at least reflect on its causes. He instead discussed digging a snow cave for the night.

In those days before affordable satellite communication, a stranded flyer's best chance was to use a line-of-sight radio to speak with planes passing overhead. The Piper's VHF radio still worked.

And so they passed the night: One person in a sleeping bag tucked in the womb of a snow cave. The other wrapped in his bag while sitting in the pilot's seat. That person's duty was, when hearing a plane overhead, to switch on the radio. Keith was on shift when a Korean Air Cargo jet passed at 35,000 feet.

"Mayday . . . mayday," he said into the headset mic while he keyed the transmitter with his left hand.

Go ahead, mayday.

Thrilled to receive an answer, Keith asked the pilot to relay information on the emergency frequency—he and Holton needed a pilot on skis to pick them up as soon as possible.

A new plan. Someone would come the next day from Talkeetna to pick them up. Keith could fly back later with his mechanic and new parts. They would fix the PA-12 and Keith would fly it back to Fairbanks.

Crashes were a cost of doing business. Keith lived through at least four of them. Once he crawled out alone with a broken leg in the Brooks Range after spruce tips caught his landing gear and the Piper nosed into muskeg.

The fabric-covered PA-12 survived that one with him, even when the trailer carrying it rolled off the Dalton Highway. With a spotwelder and some canvas skin and replacement props, Keith and his mechanic healed the plane.

He climbed out of those wrecks thinking ahead to the next step: how do I get the Piper flying again? A disabled aircraft in a remote location was another problem to be solved, not much different than a physics equation. There was always a way.

He strove to get the plane back in the air while attracting the least possible attention. There was that time his tires stuck in the soft mud of a Tanana River gravel bar. Flipped the plane on its back. Unknown to Keith, another aviator saw an upside-down Piper just south of town. He snapped a photo and gave it to an editor for the Fairbanks Daily News-Miner. Will Harrison, having read the cutline describing the red and white PA-12 that flipped on the Tanana, baited Keith with a question as he walked into the lab.

"How's your plane doing?"

"It's fine, just passed another inspection," Keith said. The less people knew of his flying, the more freedom he could maintain.

Will remembered the whiz kid glaciologist's arrival in Alaska, flush with NSF funding to study Greenland. A Caltech graduate, like Keith, Will was friends with Keith's advisor there, a man named Barkley Kamb. Kamb, a climber who had entered Caltech at 16, knew Keith's DNA.

"So how do you think our hotshot will do in Alaska?" Will asked Kamb.

"He'll be a powerhouse," Kamb said. "If he doesn't kill himself first."

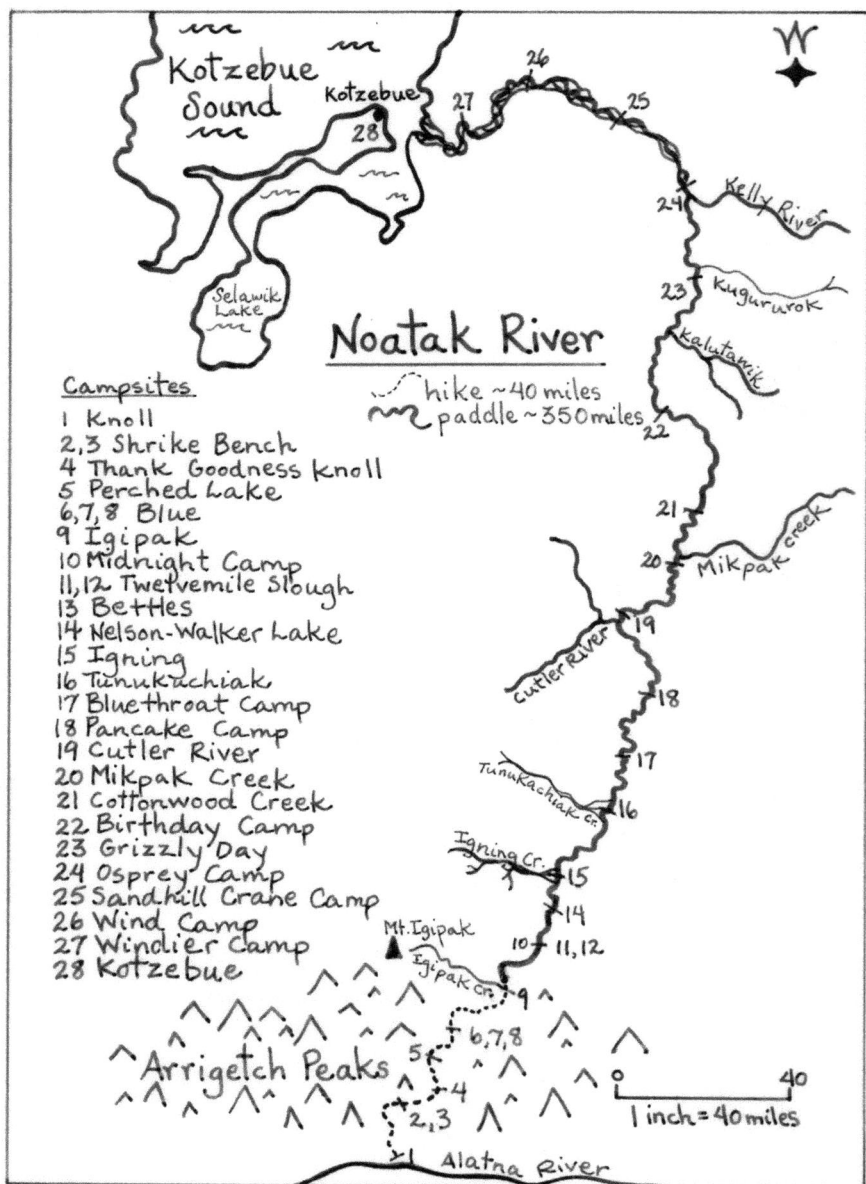

Kotzebue Sound

Kotzebue

Selawik Lake

Noatak River

hike ~40 miles
paddle ~350 miles

Kelly River

Kugururok

Kalutamik

Mikpak Creek

Cutler River

Tunukachiak Cr.

Igning Cr.

Mt. Igipak

Igipak Cr.

Arrigetch Peaks

Alatna River

0   40
1 inch = 40 miles

Campsites

1 Knoll
2,3 Shrike Bench
4 Thank Goodness Knoll
5 Perched Lake
6,7,8 Blue
9 Igipak
10 Midnight Camp
11,12 Twelvemile Slough
13 Bettles
14 Nelson-Walker Lake
15 Igning
16 Tunukachiak
17 Bluethroat Camp
18 Pancake Camp
19 Cutler River
20 Mikpak Creek
21 Cottonwood Creek
22 Birthday Camp
23 Grizzly Day
24 Osprey Camp
25 Sandhill Crane Camp
26 Wind Camp
27 Windier Camp
28 Kotzebue

5 | Great adventure

The summer plan: two people, one sled dog. One month. Hike beneath the toothy peaks of the Brooks Range, scramble up and over tight contour lines of the Continental Divide. Descend the blue thread that starts a big northern river. Stop at a stand of 15-foot poplars.

Tied to those thin stems, higher than the river will rise: a foldable canoe, life jackets, paddles. Secure in heavy cylinders tied to the trees: three weeks of breakfasts, dinners, snacks, drink mix, dog food.

July 23 to August 22. On August 23, Susan would be learning the names of nine-year olds at Anne Wien Elementary.

For Keith and Susan, the summer trip was a reason to dream over maps in the blue hush of mid-January. Keith knew smoothed patches of gravel out there where a small plane could land. The spots he would stash gear to make a month in the wilderness feasible.

Each year, mid-July to mid-August was their time. Susan off from her teaching job for the summer. Keith flying, writing, reviewing and cramming to make the time.

The Summer Trip was a difference between Keith and most other people. Will Harrison summed it this way:

"I used to kid him about how many grad students' careers he destroyed. Your normal grad student thought he could take Keith as a model and succeed. But not many people can do what he did — the mountaineering trips every weekend, flying his airplane — and succeed professionally. He had two lives, the adventure life and the professional one. And he was able to sustain both, which is saying a lot about human energy and capacity."

Holding on by her fingernails for the fantastic ride: Susan Campbell. Raven-haired, solid jaw and dimpled smile that subtracts a decade from her real age.

They met in the cinder-block stairwell of the building that housed the Geophysical Institute, where scientists study permafrost, earthquakes, volcanoes, the aurora borealis and glaciers. The institute had always been the muscle of the University of Alaska Fairbanks, due to all the money researchers brought in with their proposals. Keith was one of the stars.

Susan was new to Fairbanks. She moved there with a boyfriend. He had arranged for a short flight around their new home with a glaciologist pilot who knew the country. Recognizing that pilot on the stairs, she attempted to make Keith smile.

"Steve told me I shouldn't fly with you because you always crash."

Keith did not smile. He stared at Susan for a second and looked away. He ascended the stairs without saying a word.

That afternoon, Susan and her partner flew with Keith. They did not crash.

Years passed. Susan and Keith saw one another at moose-and-salmon potlucks that happen every weekend in Fairbanks. She told him she enjoyed the flight. He remembered her smile, the spark. He told her he was happy she flew with him. Maybe they could take another flight someday.

A late bloomer in romantic matters, Keith had chosen women who could somewhat hang with him: Helping Mindy from Caltech with her research at Mt. St. Helens just before it blew. Keri in Fairbanks and Antarctica, the high peaks of Canada and other cold, difficult places.

But things weren't going well with Keri. Susan was facing similar struggles with her boyfriend.

At the gatherings that rotated through Fairbanks cabins each weekend, they saw each other. More frequently, they were each alone.

Susan saw the roll of Keith's eyes when she asked "Where's Keri?"

They met, sometimes, for tea. They would talk and listen and sympathize. Maybe a few words of relationship advice. Maybe not.

Keith had seen what he needed. He hoped their bond could become something more. Susan did not know what she wanted. She was confused, told him she felt unfit to be in anything more than a friendship.

He thought of her hazel eyes, her dimple, as he dreamed of an excursion he could ask her on.

On September 20th, Keith participated in what was becoming a yearly ritual. Trying not to think about mile markers, he powered through the Equinox Marathon. Up and over 2,600-foot Ester Dome, through air musky with the scent of highbush cranberries. The 26.2 miles went by in less than four hours, placing Keith in the top 50 finishers.

Most of the others had run repeats up steep hills during the summer to prepare for the race, which is held on rooty forest trails with only a few miles of pavement. People have called it the second-hardest marathon in America after the run up Pike's Peak.

When the starting cannon went off in front of the university gym, Keith was seeing most of the trail for the first time since he ran the race the year before. He loped like a wolf, floating over rocks and golden leaves that hid the spruce roots. With a dim memory of the previous years, some runners could not believe that the guy in the ratty blue shorts was again passing them.

Jogging up the 2,500-foot mountain in the middle of the race, he thought of Susan. A week before the run, he asked her if she wanted to fly to Tolovana Hot Springs right after. Yes, she'd like that.

He had enough kick to sprint down the lawn in front of the

gym. He finished 30 minutes before the time he'd predicted. A smile lit his face as he saw others he knew resting on the lawn, also high on their accomplishment.

A colleague at the Geophysical Institute who had finished right before Keith handed him a cup of Gatorade. He grabbed it with his right hand while fingering the triangle finisher's patch in the pocket of his shorts. That patch meant something to him.

As he sipped his drink, Susan saw him. She smiled and came up with a hug.

With Keith indifferent to the pounding his legs had just taken, they both stepped into his pickup truck. While hundreds of others headed home for a shower, Keith would soak in a natural hot spring.

Keith drove a few minutes to Chena Marina, one of many private airstrips pilots use to avoid the congestion and regulations of Fairbanks International. After parking his truck by a float pond at the marina, they both climbed into the PA-12.

Thirty-five minutes later, they were over the spruce and muskeg Minto Flats. Someone had dozered the runway on a hill above the hot springs. The Piper bounded down for a landing. Susan couldn't believe they were there so soon. Most people drive the highway and hike into the hot springs. It takes all day.

As they walked down the hill, Keith felt a burn in his thighs, which had stiffened during the flight. He was glad to be able to loosen them and savored the pain.

After walking a narrow path through aspen trees, they were relieved to see no one was at the hot springs. They stripped off their clothes and left them in piles on a wooden bench beside an open-air wooden tub in a steaming, narrow valley.

Nervous and excited, Keith talked about his race, how good his legs felt and what a surprise that was since he had done so little running that summer. Susan talked about Tolovana, the brown leaves that still clung to the aspen trees, the smell of sulfur that always seemed medicinal.

Naked and vulnerable in the tub together, but still just friends. Keith was ready for more but had been in the game enough that he knew it was prudent to wait.

After an hour of soaking, they climbed out of the tub. They realized they forgot to bring a towel. A chilly breeze dried their bodies on the deck made of two-by-sixes. They stepped into underwear and yanked them up damp legs.

The Equinox Marathon marked the end of summer, but also the beginning of Alaska's months of quiet and white. It's a reflective time, less frantic than summer, an opportunity to think ahead.

After they dressed, they were ready for the two-mile hike to the plane. As they ascended from the springs, Keith reached over and cupped his hand around Susan's.

Their day got no more physical than that. Susan was not ready. Keith knew this, but he had a plan in place. On the walk, he invited her on an escape from the darkness of December. A trip to the Big Island of Hawaii, a common refuge for Alaskans.

This is a bad idea, Susan thought. I've got a great friend here, someone who listens and understands.

"Let me think about it."

November passed. She agonized as she woke to black windows, walked to her car after school in the beam of her headlamp. Most subarctic residents crave the tropics as the deep fade progresses. It's a gradual, innate pull toward warm, moist air and sunlight. Susan packed her bags.

She was soon on a narrow trail with a sultry breeze flowing over her shoulders. Across from her, Keith had made up his mind. He listened again to what a mess she was.

He looked in her eyes.

"What if I told you I like you just the way you are? What if I love you just the way you are?"

After Hawaii, they dated for 18 months before they married.

They were not a perfect match. Susan could not hike the ridges he could. Knowing Keri was an ice-climber and was comfortable on crumbly mountain walls, Susan told him she was no mountaineer. He looked back at her, puzzled. "I don't expect you to be."

Sometimes, when it was too steep, he would throw her a thin pink climbing rope with a loop tied in one end. She would slip her slender wrist through the oval. He gripped the other side of the rope in his knotty hand. The rope made her feel safe.

"You can do it," he said.

Though it irked him when the young bucks from the lab hesitated at crossing a waist-high creek a few degrees above the temperature of ice, he did not mind throttling back with Susan. When he needed to scout the route, she did not mind if he strode ahead, disappeared, and left her alone. He always returned with a smile and route intelligence. A few times, after thinking a bit while scrambling over rocks, he would tell her something else.

"We're not likely to grow old together," he said, referring to his life where boulders could fall, engines could quit and other things beyond human control could kill you.

She dismissed that statement every time. The law of averages didn't apply to him. Flying to Tolovana for a soak, carrying a woman over his shoulder for three miles after she had sprained her ankle in his climbing class, running a marathon without training.

She did not want average. Now, each summer featured an epic through Alaska. Each an original trip, a plan Keith hatched while flying the country and looking at the maps papering the fourth floor at the Geophysical Institute. Their trips often combined a difficult hike with a float down a river.

Their journeys covered huge swaths of the giant Alaska map. Haul Road to Arctic Village. Kaktovik to Fort Yukon. And this one: From the upper Alatna River to Kotzebue. An arctic arc that spanned the entire 425 miles of the Noatak River and the western half of northern Alaska. A wilderness distance from Boston to Philadelphia. Powered by legs, backpacks and a red collapsible canoe.

From Susan's Rite in the Rain All-Weather Line Rule, Notebook No. 391: *Arrigetch Peaks — Noatak River:*

This will be a great adventure.

It began this way: Keith, Susan and their white husky Tazlina took off with a fully loaded PA-12 from Fairbanks. They arced north over the spruce and birch of the boreal forest. They buzzed over the Yukon River, looking down to see the only bridge crossing it in its Alaska-wide swath. From there, they hurdled the Ray Mountains and headed for Bettles, a log cabin town north of the Arctic Circle.

Keith landed on the Bettles airstrip near the blue-green Koyukuk River that drained the Brooks Range, the northernmost extension of the Rocky Mountains.

Susan and Tazlina exited the plane in Bettles and walked to a nearby cabin belonging to a trip outfitter. Knowing the task he had ahead, Keith kissed Susan's forehead as she pulled off her backpack.

The Piper was soon in the air again, with Keith flying toward the crest of the Brooks Range. The stark, jutting limestone mountains would be their home for the next month.

To execute the plan, Keith needed to stash a pile of gear and food and a folded-up canoe on the upper Noatak River. He knew of a smooth gravel bar there near Lucky Six Creek, a steep waterway that flowed 10 miles from the Continental Divide.

A few hours after saying goodbye to Susan, Keith passed Mount Igikpak, a monolith 8,510-foot peak he had climbed a few springs before. He smiled at the memory of standing on top and looking out over its three small glaciers.

Passing to the west of Igikpak, Keith saw the groove in the rocky hills he knew was Lucky Six Creek. He banked hard enough to make him thankful he had no passengers, then flew over the Noatak River where Lucky Six met it.

There, the Noatak widens to one-quarter mile. Keith flew over and noted the river was not at flood stage, good, and had enough gravel exposed for a landing.

He approached the strip from downstream and downwind. As he neared his landing point, he throttled back and lowered his wing flaps. The Piper slowed to the speed of a car on the highway.

An alarm buzzed, warning Keith he was at stalling speed. He then felt the smack of big tires on rocks. He exhaled as he rolled and bounced, then pressed hard with his right leg to brake that wheel. He pushed the throttle and the Piper turned. He taxied back to a stand of thick willows and turned off the engine.

Keith opened his door and, as was his habit, did not move for a few seconds. Cool air flooded the cabin.

He was back. The deep silence of a wild, natural place: the river's gurgle and whisper of wind through the willows. The soapy smell of willow tips he had chopped with the propeller.

From the fuselage, he yanked the things they would

need, in a few weeks, to turn their hiking trip into a boating trip. Three blue plastic barrels, knee high and jammed with dehydrated meals and other foods. The green sack containing the Ally canoe-in-a-bag, along with its paddles and a small mallet for popping its ribs into place.

He heaved a barrel over each shoulder and hiked away from the gravel bar. He walked until it felt far enough. He turned left up a stream bed and headed for a patch of balsam poplar trees. They were 20 feet high, the redwoods here north of the Arctic Circle.

After packing in all his loads, he tied the canoe up as high as he could reach with parachute cord and secured the barrels to the base of the tree.

As he returned to his plane, he looked back. He didn't want anyone to see the cache. He could just make out the green canoe bag through the leaves, but the barrels were invisible from the river.

Keith was happy to see no bear tracks in the sand as he climbed into the plane. He nodded toward the cache. *See you in a few.*

He punched into the air above the silver thread of the Noatak River, which he noted with pleasure had just enough water to float the canoe.

He had one more item to stash for later use: his plane.

Their trip plan involved a long paddle down the Noatak River, which deposits its clear water into the Bering Sea. From the mouth of the Noatak, to conclude their trip Keith and

Susan would need to paddle more than two miles across the mouth of a large bay. Susan had tried not to think about that ocean crossing as they planned. Keith assured her it would be less choppy than she thought. And it was the only way to get to Kotzebue.

Kotzebue is a treeless arctic town on the tip of a peninsula shaped like a lollypop. After boating the ocean passage in their Ally Pak canoe, they would reach Kotzebue. From the beach near the town, they would break down the boat and hike to the airstrip, or hopefully catch a ride on a local's pickup or four-wheeler. Keith's plane would be at the airport waiting for them.

While flying to Kotzebue that day, Keith did not follow the northwest bend of the Noatak River, instead cutting straight over the western peaks of the Brooks Range.

He saw the red airport beacon at Kotzebue and dialed in the communication frequency on his VHF radio. To anyone who was listening, he declared he was approaching from the north.

Keith landed in Kotzebue, taxied to a lineup of similar planes and parked. He tied climbing rope from his wings to loops of rebar driven into the ground.

He then walked from his plane to the trailer that served as the Kotzebue air terminal. It was still early enough that he could catch the 1 p.m. flight to Fairbanks.

After he landed in Fairbanks, Keith jogged over to Wright's Air, on the east ramp of Fairbanks International. Yes, there's room on the 5:30 to Bettles, the woman at the counter told him.

Soon, Keith was again in the air to complete his great triangle. Fairbanks to Bettles to Lucky Six Creek to Kotzebue. From there, on commercial twin engine flights, Kotzebue to Fairbanks to Bettles. All in a day.

Upon touching down for the second time in Bettles that summer evening, he peered through his window seat and saw Susan and a white dog standing outside the log cabin. He smiled at a logistically successful day, thinking of his conveyances stored in northern Alaska.

"I wrote some letters," Susan said as she went up to hug him. Tazlina jumped up, leaving gray paw prints on the thigh panels of his Carhartts.

"Great," Keith said. "How many?"

"Sixteen."

The next morning, a pilot named Don Glazer flew Susan, Keith and Tazlina from Bettles to Circle Lake, near the upper Alatna River.

The Alatna wiggles south from the Brooks Range. They would begin their hike there. Their route took them more than 60 miles through the heart of Gates of the Arctic National Park, up and over Alaska's version of the Continental Divide.

Glazer landed his floatplane on Circle Lake and taxied near shore. He opened his door and stepped out on his floats, then into the water with hip boots. Tazlina jumped out of the plane and into the water, then swam to shore.

Keith and Susan relayed their backpacks to Glazer, who set them on a willow bush. He then took each of their hands in turn and helped them from the deck of the float to the muskeg shore.

With their heavy packs (75 pounds for Keith; 60 for Susan) off the plane, they thanked Glazer. He stepped back into his seat, slammed the door and locked it. Keith shoved his float away from shore with his boot.

Glazer fired his engine. The plane's floats left a wake as he taxied away from two people and a dog who shrunk ever smaller. Susan and Keith covered their ears with their hands as Glazer blatted past them. His floats lifted from the lake, leaving a trail of drops.

The country hissed with silence. Keith looked over at Susan and smiled.

"Ready?"

Susan nodded.

It started to rain. They pulled on raingear and shouldered their packs. Keith led them toward Arrigetch Creek, their pathway to the iconic Brooks Range peaks of the same name.

Trails, if they found them, were narrow trenches of wet peat, wounds left by caribou hooves and bear paws. The paths rarely coincided with the direction Keith and Susan wanted to go and always dead-ended for no reason.

Keith plowed through waist-high dwarf willows. Each had hundreds of leaves that held a sphere of water. Within a few steps, they were soaked to the crotch despite their rain pants. Tazlina looked as if he had just emerged from the lake. With damp fingers, they crunched wet mosquitoes in their ears. No matter. They were in love with movement. As far as they knew, they were the only two people in the world.

Their first camp was a mossy bench with a flat enough spot for the tent, surrounded by steep hills of gray rock that reached into the clouds. Holes in the mist revealed the white dots that were Dall sheep — scrappy, nimble creatures with a curled helmet of horns. Susan imagined them on those mountain shelves in midwinter, somehow scraping enough weeds to survive months without sunlight.

But now this place was alive. The hum of mosquitoes and bees, the songs of warblers and shrikes and chickadees. The citrus of Labrador tea crushed underfoot.

The next morning, and the morning after that, the rain continued. It stained the mountains black as Susan and Keith ascended the gravel of Arrigetch Creek. It soaked their boots they knew they could not dry. It made them yearn for movement and the warmth of their sleeping bags.

Despite the wet, they were both excited to reach the 7,000-foot level, where according to the map, they should have been able to see the Arrigetch Peaks, towers of black rock pictured on the brochure for Gates of the Arctic National Park.

Tazlina, not expecting visual grandeur, was not disappointed that clouds hung low, hiding the peaks. The husky pricked his ears at the whistle of marmots, high-altitude woodchucks the size of house cats. Tazlina galloped over the loose rock, so reckless that Susan wondered if they should leash her to avoid broken bones. But no leashes were the point of being out there, Keith said.

The grayness hunkered over the Arrigetch. Susan and Keith pitched the tent in the valley, made mystical by the spires poking in and out of the fog. As they settled in and boiled water for dinner, the mist descended. They could no longer see an alpine lake a dozen steps away.

Keith popped his head out of the tent the next morning and still could not see the lake.

"Doesn't look too good," he said. "We should plan on staying here today rather than moving. Get some sleep and reading done."

Susan was relieved at the plan. The descent from the Arrigetch Peaks promised the same loose rocks and the crazy steepness as their approach hike. Hop-scotching on tippy rocks was hard enough when they were dry.

So began a day of short hikes, a few naps and hours of reading. Though it was relaxing, their set-in-motion instinct had them thinking of the Noatak River, 35 miles away.

The rain's patter on the tent did not soothe Keith. Its steady beat made him envision each droplet running off the tent, through the lichen and moss to a nearby stream. Rain here meant rain just west of them, on the Noatak side of the divide. He thought of the trees that held the boat and the food cache. What if the river rose a few feet? Would the Noatak sweep away their stuff?

Those concerns melted the next day. The ceiling of clouds lifted, revealing the jagged fingers of the Arrigetch. As they ate oatmeal, they heard the screech of a peregrine falcon, and watched its jet-fighter dive toward a dodging songbird. Lapland longspurs arced above the tundra, singing their cheery mating songs on the descent. The green of the moss contrasted with the gray of the spires that rose impossibly high. The fantasy landscape looked like nothing else in Alaska. Nothing else on Earth. Keith and Susan sat back to back, feeling each other's warmth.

The day brightened. With the entire lake visible and patches of lichen glowing in the cloud-filtered sunshine, both knew it was time to go. Their stay had lightened their food bags to the point where they had begun counting dinners and snacks. They thought about the blue plastic barrels a few days away.

They crossed the Continental Divide through a nameless pass about one mile high. The pointed gray rocks they scrambled over promised catastrophe: Tazlina's shoulders rippled through her white coat as the dog braked with all four legs on the descent, starting an avalanche of small rocks.

Susan shook her head as rocks tilted under her hiking boots and her ankles shoved this way and that against wet leather. *This is crazy. It would be so easy to break a leg out here. Where would we be then?*

She looked ahead to see Keith bounding down the slope. He was skiing the scree. Susan, her toes pinched at the front of her boots, could see his dimple firing as he smiled.

Finally, the gurgle of a creek. Willows, the first they had seen for days, rose in whips, a comforting sight. Keith dropped his backpack near the trickling water, sat on his sleeping bag, and waited for Susan to join him.

"Noatak," he said. Susan smiled.

They were still 13 miles from the supplies, but reaching the river gave them both a lift. The next few hundred miles promised to be much easier, even though they were now accustomed to the weight of their packs, which had grown lighter by the day even with the sopping gear. Their food bags were as light as robin nests.

On the rocks of the arctic stream, they did not have to concentrate so deeply on their footfalls. Keith found riverside troughs burned in by caribou, allowing them to forget the 1 mile-per-hour scramble over the mountains.

As the river channel opened up and the valley broadened, they saw they were not alone. Susan stepped around a mound of grizzly scat full of seeds and blueberry skins. In the middle was the impression of a canine paw. It was twice the size of Tazlina's.

For all the beauty around them, Keith and Susan could not stay in the moment. They were closing in on the cache, which promised the delightful transition from foot to boat. And, because they were now down to a clump of humus and a few apricots, they could almost smell the macaroni and cheese.

Ten days after Glazer had left them on a lakeshore, Keith and Susan passed the mouth of Lucky Six Creek. Though the cache's location was burned in his mind, Keith still read the note he had scribbled on the map:

Boat on south side 1/2 way between Lucky Six and Tupik creeks. Look straight up gut.

To his relief, the upper Noatak had not risen much higher than when he had landed. His gravel strip was not under water. Keith and Susan felt lightness and apprehension at the same time. In this self-sufficient world, the cache was everything.

Keith recognized the gut, a steep drainage cut into a mountain south of the river. He busted toward the poplars, mentally assembling the boat, picturing Susan packing their food at the same time.

Before he reached the trees, his eye caught a splash of color. He stopped. He bent to pick up a ragged square the size of his palm. It was blue plastic.

Stress hormones boiled through his body.

"No!"

"What's wrong?!" Susan said, a few steps behind.

He held up the shard of plastic. Susan's face went pale.

They rushed toward the trees. Keith slipped on a pile of bear scat. In the mush were the remains of Ziploc bags. Similar land mines were all around.

In a few steps, he arrived at the cache. It looked like a garbage dump.

The boat bag was on the moss, in tatters. Their canoe was unrolled beneath the trees, bite holes in its red fabric. Empty bags and food wrappers littered the ground.

The three food barrels, rugged blue tubes with black screw-on lids, were gone. In all their subsequent searching, they never found a trace, except that one shard of plastic.

They had lost 20 days of food, as well as 60 scoops of dog food. The only items that resembled food were 10 bags of Earl Grey tea.

Susan cried while collecting scraps. Tazlina trotted over and licked her face.

Keith never carried a gun because he didn't want to wear the scent of arrogance in bear country, which describes almost all of Alaska. During dozens of encounters with grizzlies and black bears, he had talked softly. *Hey, I'm just here to pass through, not to hurt you.*

He thought bears could sense his calm. Maybe they did. The creatures, so incompatible with roads and cities, were something like him. Their presence helped make the wilderness a sacred place to him. But the destroyed cache was something different. A violation.

"Fuck you, bear!"

His voice echoed off rock walls.

What next? The reality of the situation: Miles from anywhere, torn up boat, enough food to last until dinner.

Breathe. Focus on the next step. Execute.

To clean up, they lit a fire. Sizzling plastic bags, wrappers and useless, punctured rubber boots sent an inky black smoke down the tundra valley. A bitter scent that drifted over the river.

While Susan fed the fire and squinted at the smoke, Keith knelt by the skin of the canoe. All the tubular metal ribs were there. And though the fabric had slashes one foot long, the bear did not carry off the roll of duct tape.

By placing the tape over the slices and rubbing it, Keith was able to warm it enough that it stuck to the fabric. The work was similar to the patching he had done on the PA-12 canvas over the years.

He worked for two hours. Susan finished tidying up. With almost an entire roll of tape stuck to its sides, the canoe was ready for a test.

Keith carried it over his head out of the woods and to the river. Susan had ferried everything that was usable to a launching point on the Noatak.

He gently set the canoe down. Susan grabbed the stern and walked it into the eddy. The boat floated.

Because most of the damage was to the front of the boat, they put more of their gear in the middle and back.

"Taz, come!"

The dog leapt into the center of the canoe. With Keith in the back seat and Susan in front, they were off, with a tentative plan.

The stress began to fade as the river took them. Aiming for the deepest water on the outside of river bends, Keith steered away from bushes that leaned into those curves. Susan dug her paddle in to pull the canoe away from submerged rocks.

As the riverbed dropped several feet at a time, the canoe splashed through whitewater, with Keith ruddering his paddle to avoid the biggest rocks. The obstacles came in quick succession, with no time off for the paddlers.

After a few hours, they saw the expected cleave in the hills to their right. As they passed Twelvemile Creek, they both thought ahead. In less than one mile was Twelvemile Slough, a stranded river channel that was now a crescent-shaped lake.

Twelvemile Slough was a common starting point for people floating the Noatak. Float planes could land there. Maybe they could wait there and get a ride out. After snacking, they had nothing edible remaining but Earl Grey and a handful of apricots.

Susan plunged her paddle off the front of the canoe just as Keith backpaddled. They executed a perfect eddy turn. Tazlina hopped out, they pulled the boat out of the water and Keith tied it to a willow.

Along a faint trail, they hiked through the brush to Twelvemile Slough. Their eyes soon caught the movement of a red jacket. There was a man and woman in their late 30s. They were shocked to see two people and a white dog approaching.

Keith waved to them.

"Hey, when did you guys fly in?"

The man told Keith his story, then widened his eyes as he heard of the destroyed cache.

"There was a party waiting to be flown in after us," he said. "Maybe you can get a ride out on the return trip to Bettles."

Keith and Susan helped the couple carry their inflatable kayaks and drybags to the river. Just as they finished and the couple was ready to launch, everyone heard the blat of an approaching plane on floats. Keith and Susan jogged back to the slough.

The pilot, who was dropping off more boaters, couldn't take Keith and Susan out in his Cessna 206. But Keith scribbled a note for him to take to another Bettles pilot.

In a few hours, in two separate Beavers that had dropped off two more groups on the slough, Keith and Susan and Tazlina were in the air, returning to Bettles.

Two weeks into their one-month trip, Keith and Susan already had a good story: hiking talus slopes through the Gates of the Arctic high country. A grizzly destroying their gear, eating all their meals and forcing them to bail.

On her flight to Bettles, Susan prepared for decompression, for seeing more people, and, when she reached Fairbanks, cars moving too fast on asphalt. She relaxed for the first time since finding the cache and thought ahead.

Keith could take a flight to Fairbanks, another to Kotzebue. He would crank up the plane and fly back to Bettles for her and Tazlina. Maybe they could camp somewhere nice for a few days on the way home. And Bettles, she knew, was a pleasant place to wait. She could write a few more letters, tell the rest of the story.

The Beavers landed at Bettles. When she met Keith again on shore, he was smiling.

"We can fix the boat here, and the outfitter says he has lots of leftover food. Says he can fly us back in. We can finish the trip!"

Susan wrinkled her brow. Then she laughed. It was amazing how different their thoughts had been. But she was not surprised. Of course he'd want this.

They had the time off from their jobs. The PA-12 was in Kotzebue. It wouldn't feel right to Keith to pay for flights to get back to his plane. Water could carry them there.

They pivoted. In Bettles, back where the trip started, the outfitters gave them leftover camping food from other parties. They purchased more, from another proprietor, with cash they had saved for a dinner in Kotzebue. Two different guides gave them glue and patches for the canoe. They bought a bag of dog food.

After staying up until 2 a.m. fixing the boat and packing the food, they pitched a tent at the end of the Bettles airstrip. The whine of a Cessna woke them at 8.

By 2:30 that afternoon, they were back in the upper Noatak country. They packed the canoe and prepared to float to their landing lake's shallow outlet and portage their gear to the Noatak. After the unexpected time around buzzing engines and gas fumes, they were burning to move.

After they got placed on the lake near the Noatak, they assembled the canoe again, ready to portage it to the Noatak. Their restart point was about 10 miles downriver from Twelvemile Slough. In the tent that evening, Susan wrote in her journal:

Just as we were getting in, three arctic loons flew in and landed 20 feet from the canoe. My breath caught in my heart.

Satin, pearl-gray heads and necks, exquisite black and white lines running vertically down the sides of their throats, checkered backs.

We decided to just camp there.

Their float of the Noatak started the next day. It was 15 miles of river they would never forget.

We heard them before we saw them, playing and howling in the willows across the Noatak.

When I saw them walk onto the gravel bar, I shouldn't have been surprised, but I was. They just appeared, slowly stepping out of the willows. Five wolves looking across the river.

They walked into the water and swam across.

We spent an hour-plus watching them, until they all laid down and seemed to be napping. We got in our canoe, smiling, and set off.

About 30 minutes later, coming around a curve in the river, there they were on a bench above us, looking down. Were they following us?

They continued on in single file. The largest one grayer than the others, the last one in line a reddish-brown. We followed them downriver until they disappeared.

We paddled about three miles down to Pingo Lake. We got out to go climb up the pingo (a circular hill with a core of ice). As we were almost around the back side of it, there they were.

One-hundred feet away. We stopped. They stopped.

We climbed up the pingo and watched them meander through the brush, the lead wolf constantly looking back at the others, waiting until they caught up.

Four wolves kept going. One just sat there watching us.

We will remember this day. We were given a gift.

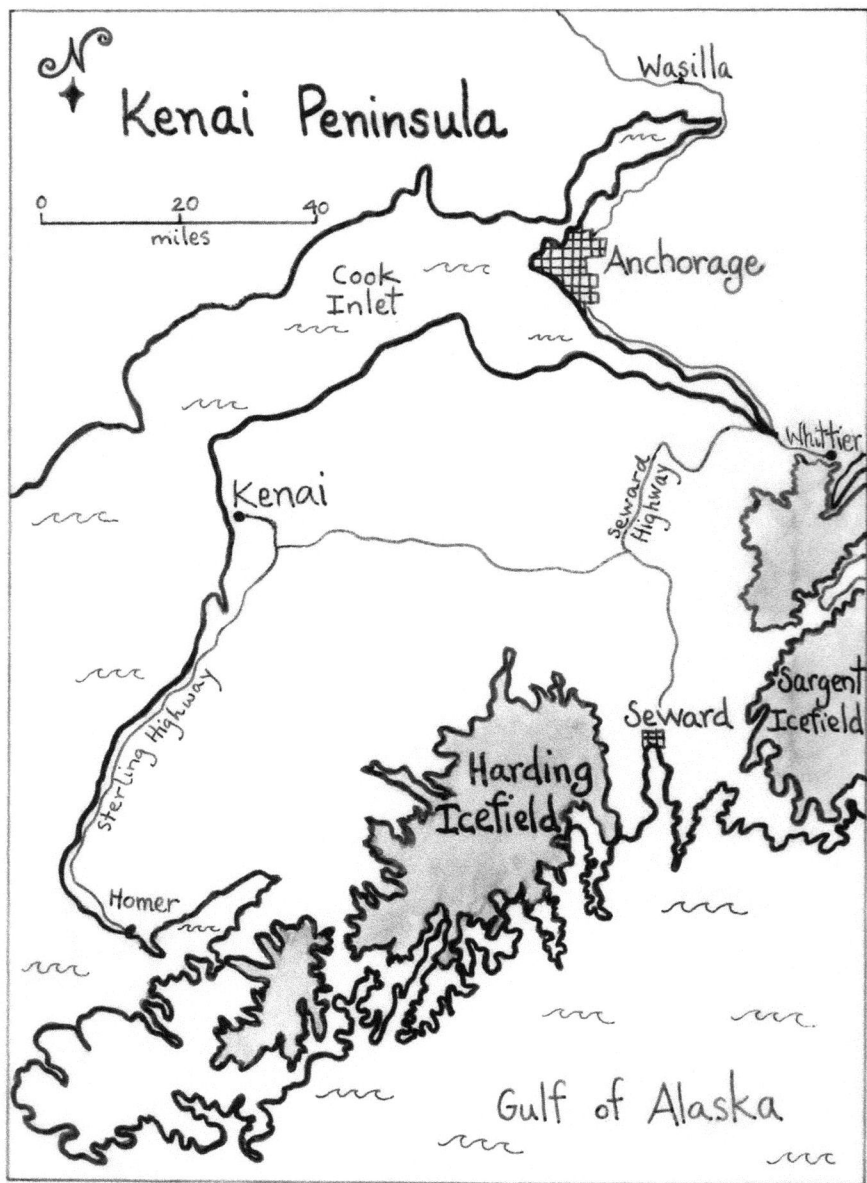

Kenai Peninsula

N

0   20   40
      miles

Wasilla

Anchorage

Cook Inlet

Whittier

Kenai

Seward Highway

Sargent Icefield

Seward

Sterling Highway

Harding Icefield

Homer

Gulf of Alaska

6 | Harding Icefield

"Let's move camp up there," Keith said, pointing in the direction of Harding Icefield. "We can get more done."

Gudfinna Adalgeirsdottir nodded and looked at Joe Sapiano. Their tents were pitched on a heap of gravel surrounding the airport in Seward, a town at the head of a deep fiord and connected by road to Anchorage.

The pair of graduate students learning to be glaciologists were helping Keith fly his profiles. He was measuring the white tendrils creeping from Harding Icefield, a frozen mass pressing down on the eastern Kenai Peninsula. Bear, McCarty, Skilak, and Tustumena glaciers were part of a busy summer: Keith would fly his Piper from northern Alaska to the south Cascades in Oregon.

Until Keith changed plans, they had flown over the icefield every day and slept on the airstrip gravel at night. Hotels were a waste of project money, he figured.

Tolly was easier for the Americans to say than her real name. From Iceland, Gudfinna Adalgeirsdottir was part of the team helping Keith profile more than 60 glaciers in one flying season. Her job was to sit in the back of the Piper and make sure laser rangefinder data was being recorded.

Her immediate task was to hike into the town of Seward with her backpack and buy food for camping high on the ice sheet. Harding Icefield, named for a U.S. president who made good on his promise to visit Alaska in 1923, covered more acreage than Rhode Island. Despite its size, the body of the icefield is hard enough to reach that most Alaskans will never see it.

"Get enough food for two days and nights," Keith said.

Tolly grabbed an empty backpack and hiked toward the Seward supermarket.

Earlier that day, while flying down McCarty Glacier, Tolly had stolen a peek away from the computer and out the scratched plastic window. The ice tongue dipped into a salt water fiord, a narrow slot left by the receding glacier. Her belly quivered when she looked down at ice screaming by, 50 feet beneath the Piper's wings.

She heard the wind whistle past the plane fabric. Keith somehow quieted the plane for the latter part of his profiling runs. She thought he might be killing the engine to reduce its interference with measurements. She wasn't sure and did not really want to know.

At the glacier terminus where the ice met salt water, she had the breathless sensation of falling off a cliff. Beneath were ice towers leaning into the ocean, then dark blue water. Within seconds, she felt the rumble of the Piper's single engine.

She breathed a little sigh. And, as always, Keith drew

another elevation line down the center of another glacier.

She never doubted him. His confidence bred trust, and she believed in him because he had no doubts.

Tolly had come to Alaska because her homeland of rock, ice and volcanoes had no graduate school. Through a connection with an Icelandic glaciologist, she had contacted Will Harrison. He invited her to an academic tryout of sorts, doing fieldwork with Keith on McCall Glacier in the Brooks Range.

Keith was impressed by her calm, confident bearing. He also liked how she spoke, with a pleasant northern European accent.

In Alaska, she was one of a half-dozen graduate students helping a world-renowned glaciologist capture three straight months of glacier-elevation flights. The laser altimetry program was at its zenith, with Keith gathering the data that would result in pinning real numbers on Alaska's ice loss.

Tolly purchased the food and walked back to the Seward airport with a full pack. Keith was ready to go, having already dropped Sapiano on a plateau in the center of the icefield.

That spot on the ice cap was 4,100 feet higher than their sea-level camp at Seward airport. One backpacking tent for three people on a plateau of snow and ice. Keith figured the efficiency of glacier flights would increase as earthly distractions decreased.

But with that ability to lift off and switch on the laser within minutes came extreme exposure. On the icefield, there was neither nunatak nor tree. Nothing to block the wind.

It came the first night — a tempest straight from the Gulf of Alaska. The tent rattled and leaned. None of the three could sleep.

After a few hours, Keith sat up in his sleeping bag.

"We've got to secure the plane," Keith said, thinking of how he could tie down the Piper so the winds wouldn't toss it off the icefield.

"Tolly, we'll need your skis," he said. "We can make a deadman out of them to tie down a wing. Let's use the car battery for the other side."

As Keith yanked out the battery used to power the computer and other equipment, Sapiano and Tolly took turns digging two trenches, one beneath the midpoint of both the Piper's wings.

Into a grave dug for Tolly's skis, Keith lowered both of them with an antenna cable knotted just above the bindings. Tolly backfilled the trench with snow, then stomped on top to set the snow. Keith tied his best bowline with the cable, securing the tiedown bolt on the wing to the buried skis.

They anchored the other wing with the battery. They also heaped snow onto the Piper's skis and patted it down before retreating to the tent.

Their tent refuge was moist, and got wetter every time they unzipped the door.

The wind strengthened. Even Tolly, quite accustomed to big winds at home, wondered how the nylon shelter could stand such strain on its seams and tie points. In his corner, Keith was doing math.

His plane could fly at less than 40 miles per hour. The wind was approaching that velocity, with gusts to 60.

"I've got to make sure the plane doesn't blow away," Keith said.

He forced open the Piper's door and entered the cockpit. Sitting in the chill, he squished his sleeping bag over his legs. He sat there, quads tensed to adjust the flaps.

For hours, he reacted to each gust, wincing at each thwack. Twilight came, and then the subarctic night. For the second night in a row, he did not sleep.

In the morning, the wind strengthened. Keith scraped ice off his window with a credit card. He looked out at the snow covering the plane's skis. Hairline cracks, but nothing suggesting the plane was ready to free itself. He saw nothing but smooth drifted snow over the battery and cross-country ski anchors. The wind set that snow to concrete. The same force that prevented them from leaving was fusing them to the dome of ice.

He winced his way out of the plane and yelled that he was returning to the tent. Tolly and Sapiano scooted their gear to the side. A few gallons of wet snow flurried in with Keith.

"How's it look out there?" said Sapiano.

"As bad as it sounds," Keith said. "We're not going anywhere soon. But I do have a deck of cards, and Susan gave me a book."

He held it up.

"Disappearance: A Map. A Meditation on Death and Loss in the High Latitudes" by Sheila Nickerson.

"That's a cheery title," Tolly said. Keith didn't laugh.

They had indeed disappeared. In the few hours of getting the plane ready after deciding to camp on the ice, Keith had not gone to town to call his wife. They had no satellite phone, technology that would not arrive for a few years. Seward had no control tower. He had not filed a flight plan since Fairbanks. By reading that document 500 miles away, someone might narrow their search for three scientists to the Kenai Peninsula.

Keith could perhaps use his VHF radio to speak with 737 pilots in a glidepath to Anchorage International, but he held that card for a bit. Hopefully the weather would clear in a day and they could break down the tent, get back to Seward and continue the flights.

The weather did not improve. The wind blew a steady 45 miles per hour. They read the book, they played cards. Tolly invented a data-checking trip that took her inside the plane and away from two stinking men for a few hours.

Upon reentering the tent to a blast of ammonia, she vowed to later remember that these were the slowest-passing hours of her life.

Even though she had purchased what she thought was an excessive amount of food, they ran out of it. They also burned all the white gas in Keith's red fuel bottle. With great difficulty, he siphoned some avgas from the wing. It's charcoal-colored smoke made the tent interior even more grim. But they had water.

"Hey, be careful with that," Keith said to Sapiano. His voice shocked the other two, because the tent been silent for hours. "Don't let the leaf get wet."

It was Sapiano's turn to read the book. Keith had noticed something on the floor: a dried leaf Susan had placed inside as a book marker. Sapiano gently picked it up and tucked the leaf in the book.

On the fourth day of being trapped, Keith squeezed out of the tent. Still a wind that vacuumed breath away, but he could see an ice chunk 40 feet away. Overhead were blue patches.

"Guys, let's get out and clear the plane. Maybe we can take off!"

Tolly and Sapiano enjoyed the sweat of digging out the skis that had been employed as anchors. Once they had them removed, they looked around and saw nothing. Whiteout conditions had again smothered the ice cap.

"Can't fly," Keith said.

Tolly looked at her freed cross-country skis. There, she thought to herself, is freedom. I can ski out to Exit Glacier! She was excited for a bit, keeping her plan to herself. Then, she looked at the topo map. The glacier was too far, the visibility too poor. And she had no food.

Another storm barreled in. Two more days in the tent. Keith combed his plane for emergency rations. In a paper bag stuffed in a seat pocket, he found a Snickers bar with a bite missing, along with a packet of freeze-dried chili. They knew the chili's vintage by its packaging: a clear plastic bag with typewritten instructions.

Keith also found a bar of Crisco lard of the same age as the chili. The Crisco would remain untouched. They ate the chili, with a third of a Snickers each for dessert.

When the food was again gone except for the Crisco, they had been atop the icefield for an entire week.

They woke on Monday morning, their seventh trapped at the camp. The storms had spent much of their energy. The sky was clearing. They once again dug out the plane.

Keith agonized. He knew he could only take one person out at a time. The Piper could not lift off with three bodies.

He looked over at Tolly, serene but tired, and Sapiano, who was smiling at the prospect of touching gravel and smelling salt air.

"Joe, take out the antenna and the receiver," Keith said. "And you get the computer, Tolly. We'll put all that stuff in the tent. We'll try to get out of here in one trip."

With the plane stripped to nothing but people, the bird lifted off for the sea. All three yelled at the same time as the skis left the snow.

Ecstatic to feel the weightless freedom of the sky, Keith swooped downward. He squinted at the wind sock in Seward and banked toward the mountains.

Tolly and Sapiano stepped out to the gravel of Seward airport. They both started laughing.

"I'm going back to get the stuff," Keith said.

In minutes, he had the plane turned around and was airborne again, heading for the hole of blue sky above the ice cap.

"Wow, not even a snack!" Tolly said to Sapiano, who shook his head. They watched the plane get smaller.

Tolly and Sapiano hiked to a restaurant in Seward. The first meal was spaghetti and meatballs, the daily special. They made two more trips to the restaurant before it closed.

That night, with Keith back in their re-pitched camp at the Seward Airport, Tolly asked what time they might be headed back to Fairbanks.

"Don't you want the data?" Keith said.

Tolly and Sapiano looked at each other. Keith turned his glance to Tolly. She had felt the hard look before. Intense, confrontational, unyielding. Like looking at a tiger.

"Yeah, I guess so," she said. "But after what happened up there I thought we might go home."

"We'll get you home after we do three more profiles," Keith said. "It's your data. You'll be happy you did it later."

Tolly hiked back to Seward again and called her boyfriend, who had first expected her back on Wednesday. She would arrive home more than one week later than planned.

There is a great lag from when information is collected until its concentrated form appears in print. A few years after the storms of Harding Icefield, Keith revised a rejected paper Tolly had drafted. He showed her his corrections and alterations. In the approved version, he listed Gudfinna Adalgeirsdottir as the first author. It was the University of Iceland professor's first published work.

The paper was more newsworthy than a typical master's project. In it, the glaciologists declared that the mass of Harding Icefield had shrunk the height of a five-story building during the past 40 years.

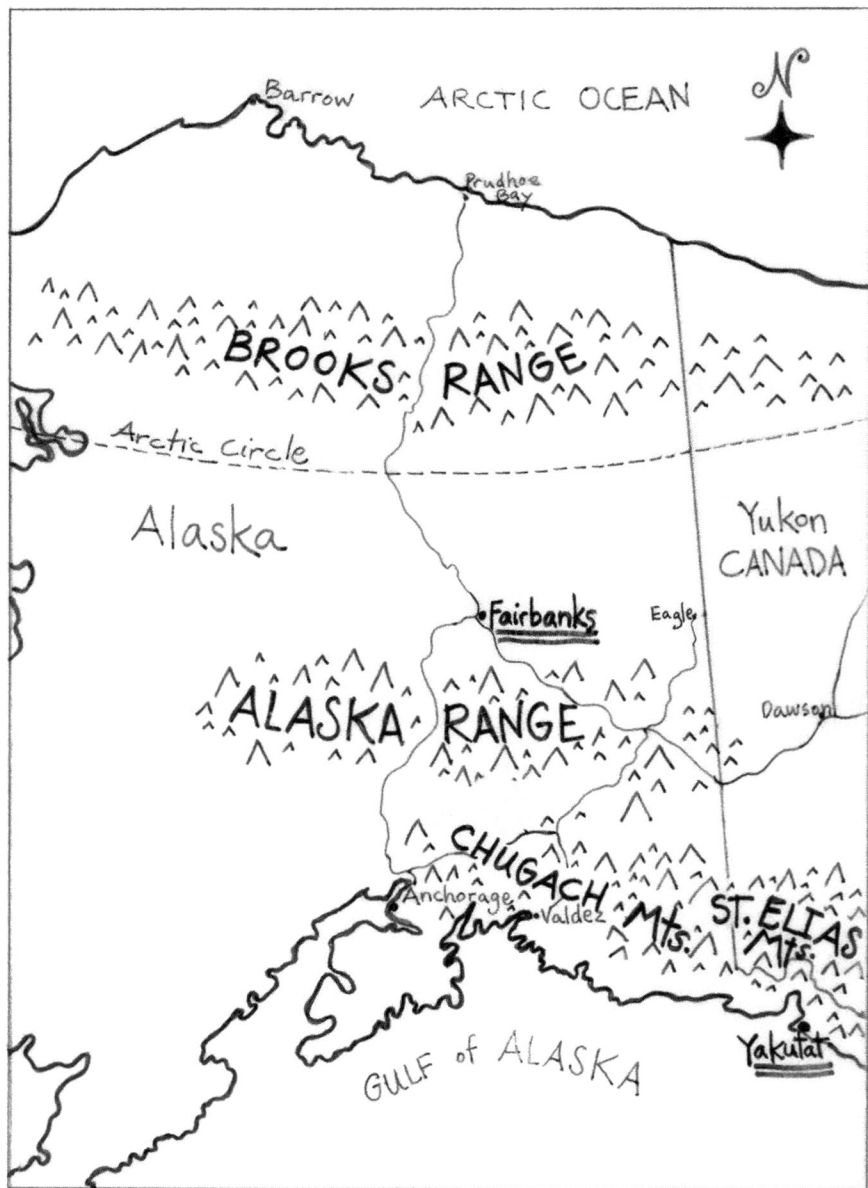

7 | Yakutat

Early June. Outside Keith's home in Fairbanks, crunchy leaves that fell last autumn, trembling new birch spades not yet stenciled by insects. Mosquitos. Sun baking the muskeg of Tanana Flats, terpenes wafting from Labrador tea.

Keith inhaled the mint of balsam, tasting it with the back of his tongue. The plants stirred on the grass airstrip after months of dormancy. He could almost hear the bursting willow buds on orange stems that reached toward the single-engine planes, wheels pressing down gravel on the private strip.

He slammed the cockpit door and grabbed his headset. The day's prospect excited him — flying a straight line from Fairbanks to the heaving North Pacific. On to the fishing town of Yakutat.

In a few hours, he'd hug old friends he pulled from all over the globe. It would be the best of reunions. Stories of bears and tents and whiteouts and sudden flashes of physics insight.

He wrapped his fingers around the control stick. He squeezed hard. His right hand worked, as it had for most of the last 46 years. Those other minutes were the terrifying ones, when the hand wasn't his anymore. Could it happen today, on the flight?

Lifting into the air, Keith climbed over the brown Tanana River. Unseen moose flicked their ears and munched greenery in the flats.

Keith arced over the lowlands with an oblique view of the country. The silver creeks and dull green spruce, as warm and familiar as the knots of his climbing trees in Wheat Ridge.

Less than one hour after takeoff, there, off his right wing, the gray/brown quilt of the Delta River, draining the big mountains to the boggy middle of Alaska. Up the chute, past the gravel haystacks, was the dirty receding ice of Black Rapids Glacier. Felt like he had just lifted the Piper PA-12 from the slush on that last flight, picking up Martin Truffer, the last man standing on the corn. They had flown around looking at slopes that looked fun to ski. He and Martin were trying to piece together a one-week trip that was not too technical for Susan and Dana.

He flashed back to the drilling project. *Should have been done. Inefficient. Can't do everything for them. Could use a few clones.*

Keith caught himself.

You can be a prick all day if you want. Your choice. The guys are doing their best.

He shrugged and forced a smile, making a point to press his face muscles against the cups of his headset. The Black Rapids ice drilling was a monster, but his charges, however gradual, were finding things of significance.

He had sent off his final revisions to the Science paper. And, most important now, he had selected competent people to set up a science conference in a fishing town. That was one detail too many. The goddamned stress.

At the restless hinge between mainland and Southeast Alaska, Yakutat, population 668, was perfect for the gathering of minds tuned to the nuances of frozen water. Ice and tides scour Yakutat's pimpled, adolescent landscape. Slowly freed from the ice age, the ground inhales towards the clouds. In Hubbard Glacier's wake, lush pungent forelands.

As Keith flew, Hubbard, withdrawn like a cat up Disenchantment Bay, was setting up for another stalk on Gilbert Point. If Russell Fiord remained Russell Lake long enough, rising waters would spill over into the Situk River, clouding it with suspended dirt and clogging the gills of steelhead until there were no more.

Surrounded by dying icefields, Yakutat would provide the conference-goers more ice than most had seen in their professional lives.

Keith could almost smell the freshness of Yakutat's cow parsnip, a plant too thirsty to live in the Interior. The day, the amazing day, made him wonder if clouds existed anywhere on Earth. If he had the power, this was the clear, stable atmosphere he would order every time he buckled in.

He whispered to himself.

Glory . . . Appreciate.

In the rattling Piper, he traced the Denali Fault, a frowning suture in the earth. A constant, imperceptible side-to-side motion powered by molten rock maintains a trench over much of the fault's length. Much of that groove is clogged with glacier ice. Here, the Canwell Glacier.

The Denali Fault had not ruptured in anyone's lifetime, but the slice was obvious enough that a generation of scientists had written papers about it. A few of those white-haired men would remember their work in a few months' time. In November, the fault would rip tundra and ice in a 200-mile line, releasing the energy of a magnitude 7.9 earthquake.

Knowing the potential of the fault from digging trenches and seeing giant earthquakes of the past torn in the soil, the elder scientists recommended setting the trans-Alaska Pipeline on 30-foot skids just south of Black Rapids. Their advice would result in the pipe sliding rather than snapping during the largest earthquake of their creative lives.

But that earthen epic was five months away. Beneath his right wing, Keith could see the section of pipeline that would skitter across rails during a few seconds of the great shake to come.

When a wildhaired newcomer to Alaska, he had hated the silver tube that slithered all the way across this place from north to south. But he had since slipped to ambivalence. In snotty skies, a whitish thread had appeared from the mist near Atigun Pass and above Shaw Creek Flats, allowing him to correct course. And the viscous syrup within the pipe funded the infrastructure that made Alaska viable. In Keith's chosen town of Fairbanks: A strong university, a half dozen Thai restaurants, an airport two traffic lights from home.

Flying over the sun-dappled flats of the Copper River Basin, Keith imagined white pinpoints of ducks and geese, as well as songbirds perched on branches. He could see the swans, regal white dots on lakes and ponds, and thought of his mom. Patty Echelmeyer's joy for those miraculous creatures had seeped into his skin, continued on to the soul. Seeing into the eyeball of a ruby-crowned kinglet while busting through brush could be the best part of a hike. *Thanks, mom.*

He thought of Patty in the Piper's back seat, on a ride to Nome to glass the bristle-thighed curlew, or a hop to St. Lawrence Island for an Asian songbird blown off course. His dad Bill, the World War II navigator on B-24 Liberators, would not fly with his son. Had a funny feeling about it.

But Patty always said yes, giggling through the gravel bar bounces. She trusted her only son's decision to visit the wilds without a gun, even though people at remote lodges thought he was irresponsible. They called him nuts loud enough Patty could hear when her son was pumping fuel. But a gun made him feel arrogant, dangerous to himself and others. He was not afraid of bears. Why should he be?

The shadow of the Piper crossed the pavement of Alaska Highway 10 as it flowed beside the Copper River. He lifted the left wing in salute to better view 16,000-foot Mount Blackburn. Seeing its blue glaciers and tabletop summit fired the image of Martin Truffer, grinning like a boy.

Just beneath the plane, a few springs past, Keith landed on a gravel bar off the road and yanked out a military duffel. Martin, Keith and Franz Mueter would later retrieve this food cache after a hike from Keith's truck to Kuskulana Glacier. They dug into the bag for their summit approach from and retreat to the McCarthy Road.

Blackburn was a bonding experience with Martin. Born in Switzerland, he was a math and physics wunderkind, just like Keith had been at Cal Tech. Deceptively tall and goofy, Martin was easy to underestimate. Maybe it was his blowdown of reddish-blond hair, or his preference for graying T-shirts and mismatched socks in sandals, as if grooming was an inconvenience that pulled from matters of the mind.

While impressing his instructors at the Swiss Federal Institute of Technology, the Swiss-German worked with Almut Iken, a woman who had studied Jakobshavn Glacier with Keith in Greenland. Sensing a kindred brain, she recommended Martin apply to the University of Alaska Fairbanks for his dissertation.

Martin had read Keith's papers and was aware of his mountaineering resume. He was intrigued that Keith flew his own plane to many of the places he studied. Like some other budding glaciologists, Martin was a climber who spent many weathered hours in his tent thinking about the complexities behind the thunder of distant avalanches.

Both knew the match was right. Keith's graduate students often received spontaneous weekend invitations to climb a peak in the Alaska Range. All of them bit. After going out with him, however, many of them busied themselves to avoid encores. Few could stomach Keith's comfort with risk, nor match his ability to minimize it by moving so nimbly. Martin was one of the few who returned energized rather than destroyed from a Sunday summit of Black Cap.

And, to Keith's and lab father Will's satisfaction, Martin took initiative. On Black Rapids, Keith and Harrison objected to few of his decisions, most of which could have been their own. Sometimes, advisors learn more from their stars than the other way around.

Keith flew into territory that excited him for its difference from the boreal swamps of home. From a distance, he saw the lumpy carpet of rocks that marked the moraine of Kennicott Glacier, and, farther on, one of his favorite human landmarks, massive red buildings leaning into a green hillside.

Scanning the wagon-road cut from the old Kennecott copper mine, Keith spotted the roofs of McCarthy. The dirt grid of streets lined with cabins of log and frame made him think of arriving there — on skis and by headlamp — a few months ago. There, under the 2 a.m. stars, he completed a wilderness trek from Nabesna to McCarthy.

The Alaska Mountain Wilderness Classic Ski Race is put on by a concrete block of a man who operates a contracting business out of his compound on the Tok Cutoff Road. A few dozen people attempt the unsupported point-to-point race each year. The roster includes some perennial names, like that of race organizer Dave Cramer. Many suffer once and never return.

Fairbanks outdoor writer Tim Mowry's "Classic" stories in the News-Miner always included tales of hamburger feet, near-misses with avalanches and charges up wrong drainages. Keith read them with a touch of cynicism. How hard could it be?

Despite his busyness, Keith signed up with teacher friend

John Carlson, who began skiing to school with a 50-pound pack. Too stretched for specific training, Keith kept his daypack light as possible on his commutes over the Skarland Trail, Tazlina trotting behind.

The 160-mile Classic was, as always, eventful. After being turned back by extreme winds and whiteout on their Plan A route up and over the mountain on ramps of glacier ice, Keith and John backtracked to the cabin community of Chisana. There, they begged some food and switched to the lowland route.

Carlson, leathery and lean, had run and hiked to a third-place in the Leadville 100 less than one year before. He trained for the high-country Colorado race by running snowmachine trails with a headlamp, once at 40 below. His bronze medal at age 40 was an unusual feat.

Despite being an ultra-running stud, John found Keith exhausting. While Keith floated the bumps like a caribou, John clawed for every mile. Depending on mood, John either marveled at or cursed Keith's flawless map-reading, route-finding and ability to ski down impossible hills.

Keith didn't fall much, but there was that time when he biffed on a 60-degree slope. He rose and dusted, ripping off a maniacal laugh. John shivered when he heard it echo off the hills.

They won the race, which meant less to Keith than proving to himself he was right; people like himself were just not entering.

When Mowry, hungry for quotes, called for a follow-up story, Keith gave him nothing: "It was a beautiful trip."

Keith later nodded in agreement when he read the words of another racer. He clipped the story and mailed it to Patty, who would understand.

"I look at it like all the parts of your body are an orchestra," said Matt Obermiller, who finished second, about a day behind Keith. "A lot of people spend their entire lives playing only a couple instruments. When I go on a trip like this I get to play all my instruments. How many things in life require everything out of you?"

Keith flew on toward Yakutat over the baby-cheek whiteness of Bagley Icefield. The view sent tingles he hadn't felt in a while. All that white space, no people. He thought of a recent visit to the Newland Street house in which his parents still lived. Without exception, all his childhood jungles in Wheat Ridge were now condos moated with asphalt. The Indian Trail was a parade of REI uniforms. And the cellphones. Why can't people shut up for an hour?

The reasons he chose Alaska were obvious now, as they were not in the belly of winter, when Susan's car battery needed a jump at minus 30. Vaulting the Bagley, he gained a view of the pancake of Malaspina Glacier. Of thousands of glaciers in Alaska, Malaspina was one of his favorites: He loved how ice becomes pancake batter when allowed to ooze. The ridiculous scale made him smile again. He remembered working on Variegated with Caltech mentor Barkley Kamb, and trying to climb St. Elias with Paul Schweizer. A true death march, that. They were lucky to escape when that Yakutat pilot was

89

somehow able to land on the quicksand mud. He thought of Schweizer's curly locks. Where are you today, buddy? Should be in my backseat.

As he saw the gray sliver of the Gulf of Alaska, Keith realized that his day of flying was one of the best ever. Pure skies, the most dramatic scenery on the planet, still somehow a secret. Now St. Elias, a pyramid jabbing the sky off his right cheek.

He imagined Susan, visiting her family in Wisconsin after the school year, was sitting behind him. He would reach back and offer his hand, feel the warmth as she wrapped it. But he would see her soon; she was due in Yakutat by the end of the conference. There, they could dream together of their summer adventure to the Aleutians: a hike through Okmok Caldera.

He banked hard over Disenchantment Bay. Just where he remembered it, the strip and its crosswind appeared as an L carved from the forest. The wind sock stretched to the southwest. Keith looped from the northeast.

Using the wind to shave speed, he touched down, tailwheel first. He exhaled as the scars spun on the black tires, then taxied to where the other small planes were tied, out of the way of the Alaska Airlines jets that arrived once each day, half full of people.

As he tied the wings of his Piper to rebar locked in asphalt, Keith realized this: He was cooked. His right hand was feeling normal, but he had an overall fatigue he couldn't shake. A Black Rapids hangover.

The rhythmic belch of a rental van with a pitted muffler pulled his thoughts outward. Someone had watched him arrive.

Martin Truffer smiled from the driver's seat. The passenger door opened with a screech. Out stepped Roman Motyka, a colleague and friend who lived in Juneau and knew Southeast Alaska and its ice.

"Welcome to Yakutat," Roman said.

"Thanks," Keith said. "The flight was pretty amazing. Wish you were with me."

"Me too," Martin said, shaking his hand. "I've heard from a lot of people who are excited to be here tomorrow."

"Can't wait," Keith said.

"You're my roomie at Leonard's," Roman said as Keith threw a duffle bag to the tarmac. "Hop in our sweet rental."

Nestled in tall, dripping Sitka spruce, Leonard's Landing Lodge is a few steps above tideline. A chill hung over their room as Roman creaked open the door after a lodge dinner of battered halibut cheeks.

They chatted a bit about how excited they would be to see their friends in the next few days, and then both crawled between the clammy sheets. Keith was ready for a full night's sleep; it was time to turn the page on the Black Rapids/conference/proposal/paper writing craziness. He was ready to bask.

But rest was elusive. Keith rolled to his right side, then his left. He couldn't get comfortable. He wished to press against

Susan's warmth.

Then, a strange sensation: Keith had the overpowering feeling he had been in the same room before. He knew he had never been to Leonard's, but the sense he had seen that same ocean view through the floral curtains was strong as it was unusual.

Then, a sudden terror. He started blinking without trying to. He was unable to stop. His right arm was next. It jerked again and again, as if he were hammering a nail. His legs kicked at the blanket. He was a marionette, moved by strings he couldn't see.

Roman woke to the sound of blankets swishing, the bed frame clicking.

"Keith. Are you OK?"

No answer. Just more unexplainable movement. For seconds that grew to minutes.

"Keith?!"

Roman's bare feet hit the floor. As he rushed over to Keith's bed, the tremors stopped. Roman took a step backward. Keith yawned and shook his head like a dog's.

"I — I don't know what just happened," he said.

"I've never seen it either," Roman said. Despite his thoughts, he said, "Maybe you're just exhausted."

Looking down in the dim twilight of 2 a.m., Roman saw Keith as he never had. Tears at the corners of his eyes. With a blanket twisted around him, his friend was a little boy.

"I don't know what's going on with me," Keith said. "But it's something. My hand . . ."

In the morning, Roman and Keith dressed. They talked no more about the dreamlike event a few hours before. A knock came at the door.

"Let's find some coffee," Martin said. "You guys obviously need some."

They shuffled out to the van on rain-soaked blue gravel. Keith tried to make sense of last night as he opened a back door.

"You drive," he told Martin. "Maybe we can stop by the dump and see the grizzlies."

"Yes, the dump tour is essential," Roman said. "It's part of the conference itinerary, right?"

As Martin swerved to miss a void in the gravel, Keith had another deja-vu. It was as if he had lived the same moment before — bumping along in the van, smelling the dried slime in the carpet, staring through a spiderwebbed windshield at wet rainforest trees.

He began shaking, as if he were naked on a glacier. Roman noticed it first.

"Are you OK?"

Keith couldn't talk. He wanted to say words, but none came.

"Can you stop, Martin? We're having some problems!"

Martin pulled over to a roadside thick with devil's club. He jumped out and joined Roman in the back seat with Keith. He felt useless holding Keith's shoulders as he jabbed and swayed. As if some demon was inside that mighty body.

"Jesus," Martin said. "Roman, we've got to get him somewhere."

"There's a clinic off the road that goes to the Cape," Roman said.

Martin jumped back behind the wheel as Roman tried to contain Keith's punching arms. As the van bounced forward, Roman felt Keith's body relax. His head slumped to his shoulder. His hair tickled Roman's cheek.

After a few minutes, Keith's head popped up.

"It happened again, didn't it?" he said.

"Yes," Roman said. "We're going to the clinic to see if there's a doctor on duty."

The nurse was drinking his second cup of coffee. Roosevelt Jones, Yakutat's only official medical care, was wondering what the day might hold. A fisherman with a hand bloodied by a winch, like yesterday? Little girl with a fever? Another visit from that woman with the sick dog?

Keith walked into the clinic, Roman and Martin following. For the third time in the past day Keith felt, somehow, that he had been in the room before. The antiseptic odor, sharp as a needle. The 1970s wood-paneled counter, behind which

Roosevelt Jones was tapping at a computer. He looked up at Keith, whom he pegged as a boat captain.

"Can I help you?"

Keith couldn't answer. His mouth was moving but no words came out.

The shaking began. This time, Keith fell to the floor. His body jerked like a shrimp. Roman and Martin dropped to his side while the public health nurse raced around the counter and joined them on the floor. Jones sat on Keith's midsection, riding him like a horse.

"Move those chairs away," he told Martin, and then turned to Roman. "You, cup his head with your hands."

Less than half a minute later, with Keith isolated on the floor, his movements stopped.

An uneasy peace returned. Roman lowered Keith's head to the carpet. All four men breathed hard, their exhalations the only sounds.

"How long have these been happening?" Jones said.

"He had one last night in the lodge and one on the way driving here," Roman said.

"What about before that? Where are you guys from?"

"Fairbanks," Roman said. "Keith flew here yesterday in his Piper."

"Holy shit!" The nurse couldn't help himself. "Does he

have any history of seizures?"

Roman and Martin looked at one another.

"I don't think so," Martin said. "Keith?"

Keith sat up, his back against a plastic chair. He turned his head from side to side.

"Can you talk?" the nurse said.

"Y-yeah," Keith said, faintly. "What the hell is happening to me?"

The nurse had seen a case like Keith's before, during his service in a village up north. But that Native man was much older.

"What's your name?"

"Keith."

"Listen, Keith, there's a number of things that can cause seizures. All of them need to be looked at quickly by someone who's more qualified than me. You need to get to Anchorage, Providence hospital. I'm going to call for a medivac."

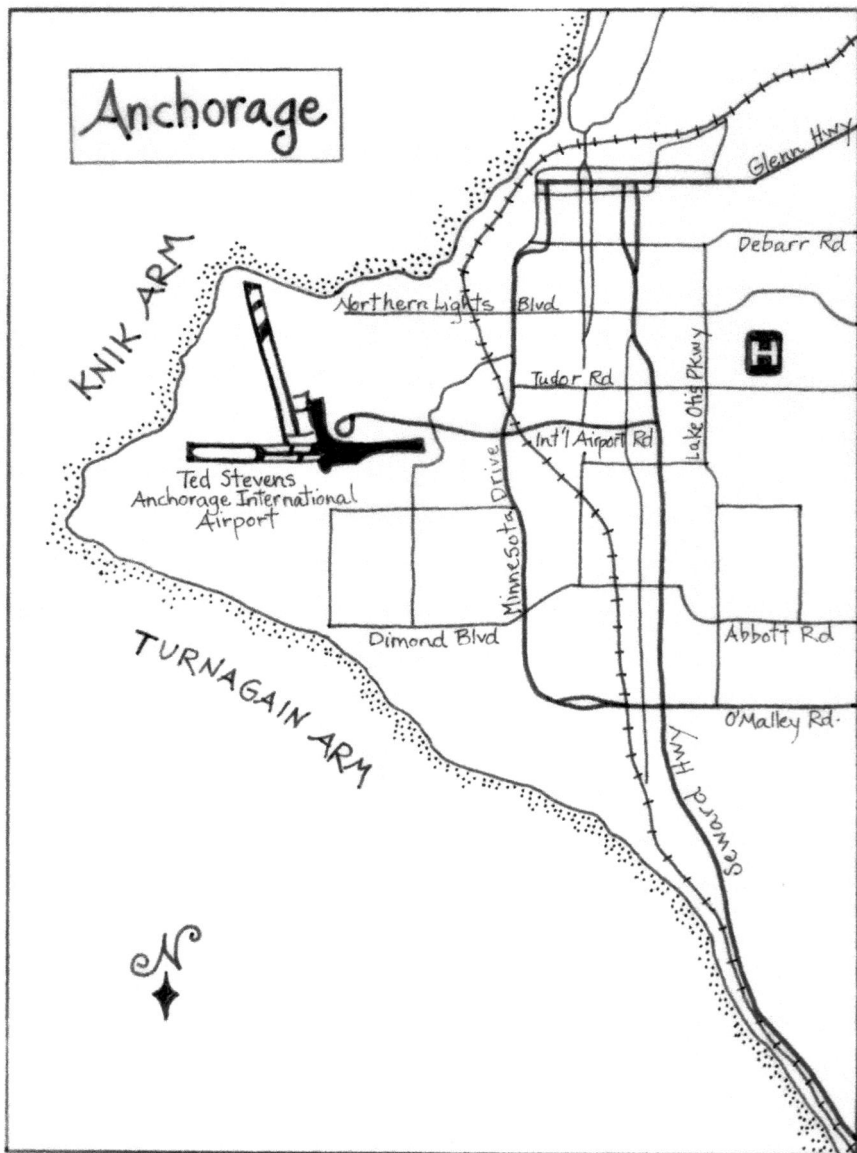

Anchorage

KNIK ARM

TURNAGAIN ARM

Glenn Hwy

Debarr Rd

Northern Lights Blvd

Tudor Rd

Lake Otis Pkwy

H

Int'l Airport Rd

Minnesota Drive

Ted Stevens
Anchorage International
Airport

Dimond Blvd

Abbott Rd

O'Malley Rd

Seward Hwy

N

8 | Diagnosis

Following Keith, Susan had busted through so many alders, swaying mid-step to avoid steaming piles of half-cooked blueberry that had just passed through a bear. She felt the electric flush of fear. Somehow, he never did.

He flew with confidence, aware of but not lingering on the mistakes. Bellying the gear into Black Rapids. Breaking his leg when the spruce caught the landing gear near Doonerak. Crawling out. The undersized trailer jackknifing when he and John Power tried to bring the plane back to Fairbanks. Leaving it on the side of the road. Flying to Greenland in a cast.

The hallway on the fourth floor of the Geophysical Institute was wallpapered with USGS Alaska maps. The entire state at 1/250,000. On the way to the bathroom, Keith would stop, rest his finger on a spot. A few days later he would fly there, dropping a food barrel 200 quiet miles from home. Alone but never scared. His excitement at seeing the spruce forest pass beneath the Piper's wheels overwhelmed the fear.

The natural world was more predictable than people. Bill Echelmeyer forced a little boy to face it: See, this trail won't kill you. These rocks won't fall on you. There's no hungry mountain lion waiting for you. Stop whining, use your feet and meet me at the top.

Fear. In Yakutat, waiting for the jet that would carry him to Anchorage. From his room in Leonard's Landing, that chamber of terrible mystery, Keith dialed the number of Susan's parents in Wisconsin. The buzz of three rings. Eternity.

With Susan's father, he forced talk about Yakutat rain. Dick knew something was not right when he handed the phone to his daughter.

She melted at his tone. Weak and unsure. Not Keith.

What an uncommon human he was. Watching him stride into tussocks at Wulik River, starting a trip. *He's so at home here.* It was the same in Australia on sabbatical. He had never been among bilbys, riflebirds, the bunya bunya trees. But he somehow knew that desert, those orange mountains.

The phone call. Minutes that shoved two lives to an unknown, unwanted bearing. He told her about the convulsing. The probable connection to his hand problem. The flight down from Fairbanks, he made sure to tell her that. *Best day ever.* Then he uttered those words.

"I'm afraid."

In the confusing normalcy between seizures, Keith joked with the pilot of the Lear jet on the Yakutat airstrip.

"Nice plane. Can I fly it?"

"No," the pilot said, forcing a grin.

The word, innocent at first, spilled through the cabin like gasoline. Glancing out the window over at the plane, secured with the climbing rope he tightened the day before, Keith was leaving a child behind. He wondered if he would ever fly her again.

At the same time, Martin remembered, less than a week ago, their aerial survey of skiable slopes in the Delta Range near Black Rapids. Was it their last flight together?

Martin sat next to Keith as Malaspina and Bering glaciers loomed beyond the right wing. Martin looked to the blue that filled the window and thought of Keith passing over the icefields on his flight from Fairbanks. If a seizure had occurred there, the chances of locating the plane would have been equal to finding a dead mosquito on the muskeg of Tanana Flats. Looking at his friend, Martin knew. *You would have been fine with that.*

But icy glory was not to be the way. Martin and Keith had spoken before of getting old, turning gray, then white. Keith, seeing the bitterness in his dad, wondered if he could take getting feeble. Or if he wanted to. During that talk, Martin envisioned Keith ambling off into the Brooks Range by himself.

Martin put his hand on his friend's shoulder. His advisor and friend, this person who turned out to be so important to his life, now seemed smaller. Older. Someone who was not, like the day before, one of the smartest, most capable glaciologists in the world.

Something happened that would never have occurred a few days before. Without looking back, Keith put his hand over

Martin's. Martin's eyes watered. He thought of Barkley Kamb, Charley Raymond and the rest of Keith's friends, moving northward. He imagined the looks on their faces as they found out.

At Providence Hospital, in Alaska's largest city, Anchorage. Susan would arrive soon. Keith dialed his mechanic in Fairbanks. He and some helpers had just painted the Piper. Maybe that bitter chemical odor that wrinkled his nose somehow affected his brain. He wanted answers. Seven rings. The mechanic was not home.

Martin sat nearby as Keith waited for the results of his MRI in a room that smelled like rubbing alcohol. A doctor entered. His words were bullets.

"You have a brain tumor the size of an egg in your head," the doctor said. "Probably growing really fast. Has to be if it's this big and you had no symptoms until now."

"What does that mean?" Keith said.

"It means you've probably got six months to live."

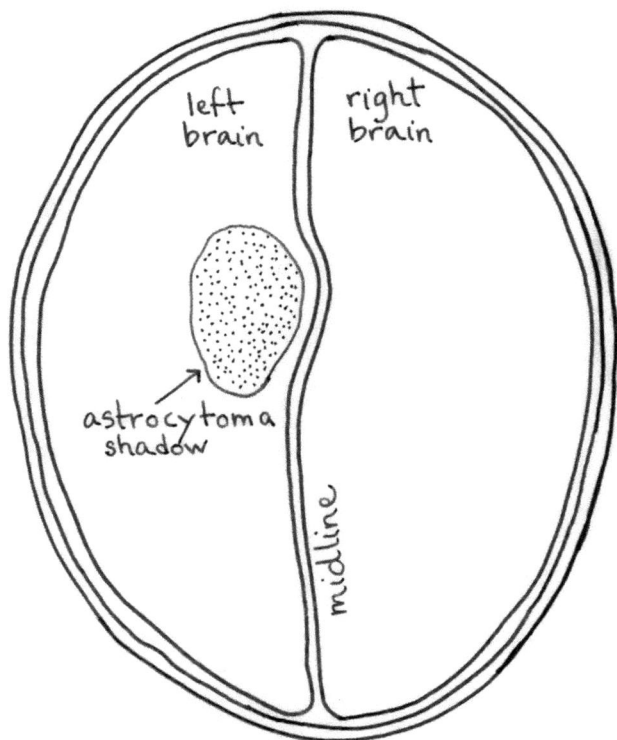

Brain Tumor

left brain

right brain

astrocytoma shadow

midline

(sketched from MRI)

9 | Cancer

Your body: trillions of tiny parcels that somehow know they are fingernail, heart, eyeball or femur. These cells prop you, turn thought into action, food into motion. Microscopic vessels containing the memory of your parents, and something new that you became.

If you are healthy, more than 50 billion of your cells will die today. In a silent miracle of industry and renewal, other cells devour them.

Sometimes, for reasons no one understands, old and damaged cells stop receiving the message. Instead of dying, they endure, dividing and multiplying, to the detriment of the mother organism.

When a person notices a lump or a strange pain, a doctor will sometimes diagnose cancer. In the eight decades available to most Americans, one in two men will contract the disease, and one out of every three women.

Cancer can occur in any group of cells. Skin cancer is the most common and survivable. Among the worst are pancreatic, liver and lung cancer.

You have a 1 percent chance of one day finding you have brain cancer. More than half of all those diagnosed with brain cancer are dead within five years.

Anaplastic astrocytoma. Keith's disease was a mass of non-dying astrocytes, star-shaped cells that are the glue-like supportive tissue of the brain. They probably do more than provide structure and bonding, but that mystery remains. Under great magnification, astrocytes resemble fluff radiating from a tiny seed, drifting on a late summer breeze.

J.M. Carroll
Cancer Center

W. Cowles St.

Airport Way

Univ. Ave

Farmer's Loop

Bellaine

Alaska
Brooks Range

Russia

Arctic Circle

Fairbanks

canada

Alaska Range

Anchorage

Juneau

Denali

10 | Radiation

"We don't really know how it works," the doctor said.

He was trying to explain radiation treatment and how high doses of focused energy can stop cancer from spreading.

Keith didn't say anything. He looked at Susan.

The tumor was taking his right hand. Reaching for an apple and raising it to his mouth was a 50/50 proposition. Sometimes he could not will his hand to grab it. Radiation, the other doctors said, could possibly halt the damage.

He and Susan were in the office of Dr. Essam Shihadeh, the radiation oncologist in Fairbanks. The doctor explained how a machine called a linear accelerator could produce high-energy x-rays. He could precisely deliver those beams to the tumor, through and around healthy parts of Keith's brain.

Keith and Susan had driven to Dr. Shihadeh's office to check their options.

"You have to do something," the doctor said. "Your tumor is growing."

"What do you recommend?" Susan asked.

"I want to treat you tomorrow."

Susan gasped.

They weren't there for action. But Keith looked into the soft brown eyes of the physician who grew up in Jordan. He felt a warmth.

"OK, let's do it."

Susan squeezed his arm.

"Good. There's some paperwork to fill out," Dr. Shihadeh said. "Then we'll image you."

"Image me?" Keith said.

"We'll take both an MRI and CAT scan of your brain. We'll find your tumor. Make a 3D map of it so we know where to focus."

The first treatment, the doctor said, was the most important. The machine would fire x-rays at the tumor from different angles to maximize exposure on the cancer cells. The goal was to bombard the DNA, the genetic material of tumor cells. Damaged cells would not divide. They died, and the body would rid itself of them as it does so many others each day.

"After one week of radiation, they start dying," the doctor said. "Radiation will shrink the tumor, stop it from growing, touching the motor cortex and affecting your hand."

"Will it cure the tumor?" Susan said.

"No," the doctor said. "But when radiation works it puts the tumor in a stop phase. . . Sometimes it starts growing again."

After finishing the paperwork with Susan's help and stripping off his clothes, Keith stepped into a white gown. He lay down on the MRI table. A large plastic donut moved into place and encircled his head. Alone in the room, he heard the metallic clicks of the machine.

The experience felt familiar, being in a space not of his choosing. A room that was at the same time restful. His mind wandered to a time long ago, but not far away.

Paul leans out of the Bibler tent one last time before kicking into his bag. Seeing the duct tape patches on his jacket, the curls spilling from his wool hat, you know he's the perfect person to share this ledge. In late July, you and the guy who really understands are the only people sleeping on Denali's shoulder.

"Lenticulars," Paul Schweizer says, zipping shut the flap. "We're in for a change."

If you were to unroll the Alaska map and select the worst place to be in a storm, you might choose 16,500 feet up on the ridge that props the south face of Denali. During the most extreme weather events, when the jet stream dips down and bulls northward, the Cassin cleaves it in two. You and Paul are on the knife edge.

The strongest wind you will ever taste arrives with the metallic whisper of the tent zipper. Soon, the Bibler quivers, as if someone is pinching the top and shaking. You half wonder if a bear, so far above the trees, is batting the nylon.

The Cassin has a few decent bivvy sites, but you and Paul did not find one. You hacked a notch into a wall of wind-hardened snow. It was like pitching a tent beneath the eave of a snow-loaded A-frame. Your perch at the top of the Japanese Couloir is almost large enough for the entire floor of the Bibler.

After spinning and growing muscle over the Gulf of Alaska, the storm unloads. Much of its energy release is frozen moisture. The tent is soon a rock in a stream. Crystals flow around, piling in the wedge of air between you and the mountain.

Paul pulls on boots and zips his down jacket to the neck. You do the same. In July, the rest of the continent features temperatures comfortable for the frailest species. Up here, the granite is 15 below.

Shoveling snow away from the tent warms the body's core, but the wind jerks you toward the ice chute of the couloir. You stagger into the tent.

Two feet from your ear, Paul's lips move but you hear the wail of tortured fabric. His back is against the uphill wall, heels dug in, quads burning inside his sleeping bag. You shove boots in your bag, wincing at the wetness, and turn your back to the growing mass a few millimeters away. The physicist in you is fascinated with the weight of so many tiny six-sided crystals. Feels like a cold sack of flour.

The four-pound yellow Bibler, your old friend. Thin as arrow shafts, those crisscrossing poles. How many pounds can they take?

Under two feet of snow, with muffled pings, the poles relax. The tent drops like sweaty folds of sumo flesh, pinning two bodies on a face of cold rock. It is 3:30 a.m.

With the information from the MRI and CT scans, a technician created a three-dimensional diagram of Keith's brain. The tumor webbed over his left parietal lobe, which is why it was taking his right hand. His head, shown as a map, made perfect sense to Keith.

With a few clicks, the technician colored the blob red. Turning it this way and that, he conferred with the doctor regarding the best angle for the x-rays to penetrate, the point of entry that would minimize damage. Complicating this was that no doctor had operated to remove any of Keith's tumor — all agreed the surgery would kill him. Radiation is most successful as a clean-up procedure, removing remnants after the tumor has been cut out.

"We'll need to fit you to a mask," Dr. Shihadeh said.

"Mask?" Keith said.

"To make sure you don't move during the treatment," the doctor said. "You'll look like a hockey goalie. We use it to secure you to the table."

With tent collapsed and the air pressed from your lungs, you agree with Paul: kicking and screaming trumps buried alive. The Bibler is gone. You've got to get out. Now.

Chaos. Prepared as one can be for this terrible event, you are wearing all your clothes in the twilight. The subzero air burns like fire. Paul is yelling in your ear but you can't hear him. He's not wearing his gaiters. Everything's buried.

Got to do something. Pawing the snow like a dog, Paul mines the yellow nylon, emerges with a shovel. The snow, too new to sinter, piles in dunes. As soon as the blade removes, the hole fills. The supply, flowing from above, is infinite.

No snow cave here. Don't want to know the wind chill. You are now sure of one thing — if you don't get out of this blow, your bodies will join the dozens fused to this mountain. Their last panic must have tasted like the pennies in your mouth.

A nurse soaked a special sheet made of cloth and plastic in warm water. She walked over and pressed the sheet to his face, folding it gently over his nose. Then she moved her hands to the edges. The material stretched over his face like a washcloth.

"Give this a few minutes to set up," she said. I'll be right back."

An ice cave. You and Paul rappelled over a cornice and found a brittle wall of ice. Hours of chopping with axes. The result: a silent womb of protection that fit two climbers.

Slither inside. On your back, panting. Adrenal glands squeezed dry. A full day since food, drink.

Paul went back up to fish out your Coleman Peak 1. He couldn't find the tube of preheat goop at the bombsite. Hell of a mountaineering stove. Why did you bring it? Without water, you are dead. Paul curses and keeps fiddling.

"Strange," Paul will later write of this moment. "This wretched little hole will be the scene of my last battle on Earth. Guess it had to happen sometime."

You fall into a dream. Paul, your college buddy, your field assistant on Blue Glacier in Washington, so long ago. Skinny, ripped, owl glasses, hair halfway to his butt. His blond girlfriend up there, what was her name? Hot. He the philosophy major, on his way to professorship somewhere. The big ice sheets call your name. You both agreed, way back then. High-level academics and world-class climbing. Few people in this world can do both. Over beers, the conviction: no buckling to conformity. The vow: to remain different. You had the immense talent and energy to pull it off, right?

You are 33 years old. Six-one, a lean 200. A body that answers all the absurd demands. Staying up all night on McCall to get the sensors placed on the ice. Skiing to work with Tazlina. Tagging a first ascent in the Brooks Range no one will ever hear about. Life is training. The machine is always tuned.

Trying not to set himself on fire, Paul keeps sparking the stove. You wake occasionally, mistake his breathing for Taz's. Don't want to think of what will happen if we can't put the brew on.

Someone is yelling in your dream.

"Fuckin-aye! . . . Yes!"

Eyes blink open. Paul has done it. The sputter, the purr of the Peak 1. Designed for picnic tables in Michigan, this one coughs to life in a dank grotto on top of the continent. The sun-yellow flame melts to blue. The hum of salvation.

Paul lifts clear ice chunks into the pan. They transform, so slowly, to the stuff of life. The smell of ether and steam. Such a little thing, the mug of instant chicken noodle. Up here, life itself.

"The mask should be set up now," the nurse said.

She pulled off the sheet, which was then white mesh with the contours of Keith's face.

"What are those holes for?" he said, noticing the base of the mask.

"We put bolts in there to secure your head," she said. "We can't risk you moving when the machine is on."

Susan, sitting next to Keith, thought the mask medieval. My God, she thought. What's next? Leeches?

The next day, Dr. Shihadeh ushered Keith and Susan to the room containing the most expensive and precise instrument located in the city of Fairbanks, Alaska. Ready to concentrate within Keith's head the invisible particles that made Japan surrender in World War II. Harnessed by human ingenuity.

The door to the radiation room, with its hourglass warning symbol remembered from bomb shelters when Keith was a kid. The door belonged on a castle wall. Four inches thick, hundreds of pounds of lead. Balanced on massive hinges. The radiation room was encased with three feet of concrete. To prevent the x-ray beam from reaching anything but the patient.

Keith laid flat on the table. The nurse positioned him. She then lowered the mask over his face. Red laser light shone on the mask. The nurse drew on the mask with a red Sharpie, sketching a bulls-eye.

"We'll have to leave now," Dr. Shihadeh said to Susan. She

squeezed Keith's hand. Stretched on the table, bound by the mask, he looked like he was about to be tortured.

"You probably won't feel anything, but some people say they see a blue light," the doctor said. "We'll see you in 20 minutes."

The doctor swung the chamber door shut with a thick echo. Keith lay there, bolted to the table.

Outside the heavy door, Dr. Shihadeh touched Susan's shoulder.

"There's a waiting room over there," he said.

"OK, she said. "But I'd rather be here."

She sat on the polished floor, back against the chamber door, a few feet from where red laser light focused on the cheek of Keith's mask.

The cave warms and drips. Belly wants more than two cups of soup, but the storm of the decade roars on. The mind screams ration. Inside, the peace and warmth of a sauna. Hard to tell wake from sleep. Paul's silent. Words are a waste.

Three days. The monster won't die. Food dwindling. Paul tacks a plastic compactor bag at the entrance hole, to keep the snow out. Strength to chop, so you do, feet in your sodden bag. Squint at exploding ice. After a hack, something familiar in the wall. Green wool.

A glove.

"There's a body in here!"

Paul stirs, joins the excavation.

No corpse, just a glove, but more human artifacts. Etriers with wooden rungs. Coils of braided rope. Stashed, abandoned, years ago. Then, something useful. A glazed brown paper bag with Japanese letters in black marker. Inside, desiccated grains of white rice. About a pound.

"Maybe this stuff was left by the original Japanese Couloir team (from the second ascent, six summers after Cassin's). Looks like the right vintage."

The next morning, the storm shifts from the mountain, lumbers toward Kuskokwim flats. Shocking skies when you shove aside the compactor bag. Had forgotten the color blue. A piss, outside! Standing, blinking at the white.

Back in to yank out what remains. Transfer the rice, now the only food, to a stuff sack.

Upclimb. The only way out is up. The Valley of Death almost lived up to its name on the way in. A mountain of ice avalanched, too close. Can't go back there again. Besides, in your alpine approach you only carried one rope between the two of you. Need the relative stroll of the West Buttress route for the descent.

Denali's summit is anticlimactic — on a platform of white the size of a sheet of plywood, the smell of wet snow. You just want to get the hell down and find your food cache.

You found it before the ravens, the best tasting jar of peanut butter on Earth. You and Paul paw it like bears until the jar is empty.

As you are eating, the whine of an engine. The air taxi pilots wags his wings. He will land upglacier. On the largest mountain in North America. Just 100 miles from Fairbanks, from the office of Dr. Essam Shihadeh.

The lights flicked on in the radiation room. Keith blinked. The treatment was over. The nurse appeared, ratcheting out the screws that held the mask. The clicks were a metallic cricket in his ear.

The nurse lifted the mask from his face. He saw Susan's dimples. She bent down and kissed him on the cheek.

Rapid Wastage of Alaska Glaciers
67 surveyed glaciers in seven geographic regions
(18,000 km²)

Brooks Range

Alaska

Alaska Range

Yukon

Wrangell
Mts.

St. Elias Mountains

British
Columbia

Chugach
Mountains

Coast Range

Kenai
Mountains

Gulf of Alaska

N

Kilometers
0   200

11 | Rapid Wastage of Alaska Glaciers

We have measured volume and area changes on 67 glaciers, representing about 20% of the glacierized area in Alaska and neighboring Canada.

Our ... estimated annual volume loss is nearly twice that estimated for the entire Greenland Ice Sheet during the same period.

Alaska's glaciers have, over the past 50 years, made the largest single glaciological contribution to rising sea level yet measured.

The most important paper came out July 19, 2002. A few short months after Keith's final flight to Yakutat, in the most unsure time of his life, came the high moment of his career. His study was based on work he could never repeat, because the brain tumor no longer allowed him to fly.

Keith received the email about the study's upcoming publication date on a day he slumped through chemotherapy. He hugged Anthony Arendt the next time he visited the lab. It didn't seem fair that after so much work, the reward that followed was muted by daily circumstances, like the sensation as warm shower droplets burned his skin like acid.

When he received his preview copy of the issue, Keith felt a jolt. The featured study that week was a neurological advance. The purple-stained image of a brain filled the cover. The brain belonged to a lab mouse.

Halfway inside the journal was black and white proof of his life's passion. Four pages of text, including a map of Alaska glaciers flown and a few simple graphs.

Thousands of Alaska glaciers are the resting place of snows that fell yesterday and many years ago. Those ribbons of ice worm along in curving trenches between mountains from sea level to 20,000 feet. Almost all of them are shrinking fast. Alaska's glaciers are dumping as much melt water into the oceans as Antarctica is, despite being one-eighth the size.

In an opinion piece written for that same issue of Science, Mark Meier of the Institute of Arctic and Alpine Research wrote that Keith's results meant that Alaska glaciers contributed half of the world's glacial sea level rise. This despite Alaska being the home for only about 13 percent of the world's glacier area.

Why is Alaska's ice so significant? In contrast to polar glaciers that have colder ice, many Alaska glaciers are low-elevation tidewater glaciers that spill into an ever-warmer ocean and melt faster because they are touching that water. And a striking warming trend in Alaska air temperatures not only has been melting glacier ice. Warmer air is making more rain and less glacier-nourishing snow. Some Alaska glaciers, like Yakutat Glacier, are dying, with not enough snow in accumulation zones up high to overcome melting at sea level.

Because the study appeared in Science and the members of its public relations team crafted a press release, reporters bit the hook of legitimacy. In the July week the study was released, Keith and Anthony answered calls from reporters for the BBC, Washington Post and New York Times.

Keith deferred most of them to Anthony, who Keith decided should be first author, as he had with Tolly on the Harding Icefield paper.

One year after his diagnosis, Echelmeyer and By Valentine hosted Alan Alda of Scientific American Frontiers. The likable host and actor had many scientists to visit on his short trip to Fairbanks. He did not ask why the glacier expert's scalp was showing through his curly hair, nor why his face was bruised and puffy.

Alda's cameraman focused on Valentine, who said the amount of water shed from Alaska's glaciers since the 1950s was enough to cover the state with seven feet of water, and enough to put Texas 15 feet under. America's largest state had by itself raised global sea level by more than one-quarter inch in the last 60 years.

ALASKA

Fairbanks

CANADA

CALIFORNIA

Commonweal
San Francisco

COLORADO
Denver

12 | Commonweal

A life-threatening illness warns us that the end of this life may be closer than we had thought. And with that sense of immediacy comes a transformation — a knowing of the work that matters to us now — the work that remains to be done. There is no time to waste.

So wrote Michael Lerner, founder of the Commonweal Cancer Help Program. Commonweal is a retreat center on the Pacific coast a few miles from Bolinas, California.

Keith and Susan spent a week there north of San Francisco at the breezy, green plateau of stillness above the Pacific. Commonweal is for those who think there might be something more to healing than traditional Western medicine. A place for wondering, mourning, learning.

The curriculum: Yoga, meditation, deep relaxation, counseling, good food and learning how to prepare it, massage. Joining seven strangers faced with the same uncertainty. Speaking. Listening. Pondering death.

Retreats are held six times each year on 60 acres within Point Reyes National Seashore. The eight guests stay in Pacific House, one of several Art Deco buildings on land that once housed an RCA and Marconi radio transmitter site.

Michael Lerner, 75, a political scientist by training, in 1976 founded Commonweal, a nonprofit health and environmental research institute. After Lerner's father was diagnosed with cancer in the mid 1980s, he started the Commonweal Cancer Help Program. He designed it to help people answer the question attached to every diagnosis:

Cancer has transformed everything. It takes you into a world that is fundamentally different from what your world was before. And it asks you: how shall I live now?

For Keith: How to keep on? So much lost, in one day. Expert on masses of ice flowing from unpeopled mountains, telling a story of the world. Flyer of ice and forest and mud and ocean, feeling the Piper PA-12 through palms and gut. Owner of a resilient muscle-and-tendon vessel that moved over scree slope and powder snow with animal sureness. A mind that processed landscapes and equations with unusual speed.

There are no televisions at Commonweal. No radio, no computer access. There are pelicans kiting the wind in formation, deer, fog, the tang of pine sap from branches broken in storms.

At Commonweal, Keith and Susan met Waz Thomas, a tall, thin, graceful black man who had been there since the cancer program started. He was their yoga teacher and the facilitator of group discussions.

"Do any of you have a guess as to how many people will die today, worldwide?" he asked eight people gathered in the airy

Pacific House.

Keith, Susan and six others looked at one another.

"One-hundred fifty-five thousand," Thomas said. "Somewhere in the world, a person dies every two seconds.

"There. We just lost two more.

"I'm not telling you this to scare you. I'm pointing out how natural death is. In our society, we tend to shove death into the basement. We're talking about death here not because cancer equals death, because it doesn't. We just want to take a flashlight and shine it down into that basement."

Keith thought about death, as he had many times. To his scientific mind, death was the ultimate curiosity. A problem common to everyone. Mystery with a capital M. Sort of like all those unanswered questions he had in the wilderness. How can a godwit fly for seven days? Why did Black Rapids run toward the highway in the 1930s?

Thomas encouraged quiet contemplation after the session. Susan walked back to the room in Pacific House.

Keith chose to hike on a soil path on the clifftop. Alone, he came to a cedar-shingled structure known as the Meditation Shed. He slid the wooden dowel that served as a door bolt. He stepped inside onto soft wicker matting that covered the ground. There was a low wooden table filled with rocks upon which people had written messages to loved ones.

He squatted and then sat down. He looked out through the open door, watched the cypress trees lean into the breeze. He smelled the salt air.

"The sacred crisis that accompanies cancer is one that shakes the settled experience of identity to its core and invites a renewed curiosity to explore what may be arising out of this time of illness," wrote Francis Weller, co-leader of the Commonweal program. "The healing process associated with serious illness instigates a move within the soul to address all the untended wounds that have accumulated over a lifetime."

On the California coast, Keith closed his eyes and remembered back to that time in the hospital, just after Yakutat. Susan was there, having flown the shortest path from her parents' house in Wisconsin.

"Are they coming?" Keith asked her.

From Wisconsin, she had called Patty and Bill in Denver, telling them Keith was sick.

"Yes, they get in later today," she said. "Getting a rental car and heading right here."

Bill Echelmeyer had visited Alaska before. A trip on the Noatak River, of Keith's design. Bill groused about the lack of meat in the meals his son planned, but enjoyed the thrill of rafting through wild country. Another trip, with Patty to the Alaska Peninsula, canoeing with Keith in big wild lakes. Having a lake all to themselves; hard to experience in Colorado. Their guide: a son who knew the place despite never having dipped a paddle there. The kid was in his glory. Strong and fearless.

Bill had started it. Arrowheading, mushroom hunting, mountain hiking. Every weekend with the kids, something outdoors and physical. Bill introduced Keith to the mountains. When he was 5 they started hiking the Indian Trail just outside Denver, overlooking the town of Golden. On a similar trail he told his son "See you at the top," and left a 12-year-old whimpering behind.

The young Keith responded. He could do it, just as he later could climb ice walls using ropes and picks. Just as he could get caught out at 40 below zero and survive. His father set no boundaries on Keith's comfort zone. It expanded with each of his son's experiences.

In the Meditation Shed, Keith remembered back to Providence Hospital when Patty hugged her son's head. Tears pooled in her eyes. Keith, 46, was again the boy in his wet tent who needed answers. Bill, feeling helpless and suffocated, clasped Keith's left shoulder with his hand.

"Thanks for coming," Keith said. "I don't know what's next."

Tears lined Patty's face. Bill squinted. What could a parent say? Do?

After a few hours with Keith and Susan, Bill and Patty left the hospital. They needed to find a hotel room.

On the drive through the noisy Anchorage grid, Bill felt an impulse.

"There's nothing we can do at this point," he said to Patty. "Let's use this car to get out and see some Alaska. We're just in the way with all his friends coming here. Let's give him some room and see him in a week."

Patty was incredulous. How could they leave Keith?

Bill would not bend. Patty was crying, shaking when they drove away from her son.

They toured the Kenai Peninsula for six days, looping from Anchorage down to Homer and back. The eagles at the Spit and white volcanoes from Clam Gulch gave a few minutes of pleasant distraction. But their thoughts always came back to their boy in that hospital room. Such a foreign, unexpected place.

Many of Keith's friends and colleagues visited his room at Providence. The Yakutat conference-goers all had plane connections in Anchorage. They stopped in at the hospital during layovers. But where were his parents?

The wound, pressed again through the gauze of time. He felt its familiar sting.

His father was, more often as he grew older, so bitter. Keith had inherited much of Patty's sunny disposition, as well as his father's German flint. But he found some of his dad's actions hard to understand.

Now, in the 8-by-10 foot shack above the Pacific, Keith was in a new state of uncertainty. One that embraced mystery and awakened compassion. He tried to imagine what Bill's life was like.

He remembered his dad shaking his head, refusing to fly with him, saying it didn't feel right to climb into his son's plane. *Why not? You flew in B-29s in the war.* Or the times Bill growled at him to get a haircut or at least take a damn shower.

What made him so mad about my hair? Keith closed his eyes and tried to imagine himself in his Dad's place.

More than anything, Bill wanted to be outside. As a teenager growing up in Philadelphia, he enlisted in the Army Air Corps for duty during World War II. He was a navigator in a B-29 Superfortress bomber. Bill loved to fly and to read the compasses, gyroscopes and radar, keeping the pilots on the right path. Out of his small window just behind the co-pilot, he and his crew snapped photos of Japan a few months before another B-29 dropped the atomic bomb on Hiroshima.

After the war, his grades in high school and help from the GI Bill got him into Penn State. He wanted a degree in forestry, envisioning days on pine-scented mountain slopes.

At Penn State, Bill met Patty, the English literature major and smiley delight who married him. He moved west to Casper, Wyoming with her, then to Colorado. In the space that came with the 1950s West, he could breathe where the plains met the mountains.

Keith's sister Randy Sue was born in 1951, when Bill was 29. Keith followed three years later.

Bill and Patty bought a house close to downtown Denver. Bill got an offer for a job at a bank, as personnel manager. The pay was good. He had a family. He took the job.

There, looking from the bank window, westward to the purpled mountains, came the disappointment. So close, but living in a growing urban center that attracted people for the same reasons he came. His spirit ached for the hills. But most of Bill's hours were not spent in them.

Young Bill had envisioned his days in the woods, breathing fresh air, working hard and collapsing after a good meal each night. An office job was not what he wanted to do. But it allowed the kids to go to good schools, to have what the other kids in Wheat Ridge had.

The responsibility, the sacrifice, the loss of identity that follows parenthood. *How shall I live now?*

Keith could feel his father's jealousy. Like every child, he had not thought it possible. His parents visited at Caltech, at Blue Glacier on Mt. Olympus in Washington. They saw their bronzed son climbing snow peaks, flying glaciers, landing on ice. Bill was always so critical of the scientific papers Keith had authored, not detecting the soul behind the science. *How am I supposed to understand this?*

In the reflective space of the meditation shed, Keith once again faced the choice of which feeling to feed.

He put a hand to the red bandana wrapping his forehead: Friends wouldn't blame him if he stopped talking with his dad, who had once driven away from a crying boy, leaving him to think about his behavior on the side of a highway. Who ran rather than be at his side in the hospital.

Victimhood is a powerful mask. But Keith needed to turn away. He decided to turn toward his father, build a bridge. *There is no time to waste.*

Appreciation was the tool. Keith wrote this letter to Bill and Patty from Alaska when he was 32:

The other day when I was coming home from climbing Mt. Deborah I got to thinking what an enjoyable and interesting life I was having and how lucky I was to learn to appreciate the outdoors and wild, natural phenomena, hiking in the woods, high mountains, rivers, trees, and flowers and animals and birds — and close friends to share them with. Dad, even though the two of you might not have instilled your enjoyment of some things — cities and history and religion — into me, I owe my interests and feelings and the ability to pursue them to you. Your teaching when I was young, your own excitement and interests, the freedom to pursue things, support for my adventures, college . . . I'm not very good at saying all this, but thanks for all you've been to me and how you've helped me grow.

A few years after visiting Keith in the Anchorage hospital, Bill was diagnosed with multiple myeloma, a form of bone cancer.

After they heard the diagnosis, Keith and Susan traveled to the house on Newland Street. Unable to climb stairs, Bill stayed in Keith's old bedroom, a tiny space on the north side of the house. It was the same room in which Bill had encouraged his son's interest in chemistry by building him a small lab, installing a gas burner and buying him flasks and powdered chemicals.

During the visit, Patty made Susan tea. The two of them chatted in the living room amid Bill's maritime artifacts and framed arrowhead collections.

Through the wall, they could hear Bill's and Keith's voices. Sometimes soft, sometimes yelling. Two men with cancer, working it out.

Keith would stay in the room for hours with his dad, who died at 83, not long after those sessions. Reconciling, healing. Realizing his dad, despite the bluster, was proud of him. Letting Bill know, before it was too late, that he loved him.

SKARLAND
SKI TRAIL

13 | Skarland Trail

How can he take it? Jon Miller wonders, watching his friend's body thud to the snow. *This was a bad idea.*

Keith is trying to ski one of his routes. The Skarland Trail curves through forested hills and crosses three roads as it leads from Musk Ox subdivision to campus. Keith skied it dozens of times, often with Tazlina, on those glorious, increasingly rare days he did not have to visit the plane or sit in a committee meeting or haul trash.

Springtime was best. After the volunteer groomer had fired up his snowmachine and towed his tracker, which left a set of perfect, parallel grooves. Tazlina's feet would mess up the tracks a bit, but so it went. Some fun dips and rises through birch, prickly rose and spruce.

Like weeds in the garden, houses keep intruding. Shoving the trail in spots and adding a heavy perfume recognized as dryer exhaust. Even in Alaska, people want a nice place to live.

On a warm day, before, Keith could ski the four miles in one hour. Now the trail goes on forever.

Pow! Down goes Keith. His climbing helmet tilts, but did

not take the hit. Right shoulder this time. A meaty sound when muscle meets packed snow. Another purple bruise.

"You alright?"

"Yeah, I'm OK," Keith says, shaking as he presses to one knee, using his ski poles to rise.

Wobbling. Teetering. He steps back into the tracks. Leans over his poles. Pushes down the trail. Clumpy wax catches on birch seeds shaken loose by redpolls. He pitches forward, smacks the trail again. This time, the helmet connects. Blood runs from his left nostril, runs through his mustache to swollen lip. He tastes salt, looks up at Jon with the eyes of a boy.

Jon thinks he is being irresponsible now. *Jesus. I'm going to kill him.*

Like Shad did when Keith asked to go rock climbing again — don't tell Susan — and got stuck on the wall, unable to go up or come down. *What do I do now?*

This time, Jon does not offer his hand. It's a brand-new world. Keith is now pulling the food bag from his pack, handing over the extra weight.

Keith does not want Jon's hand. He wants to get up on his own, no matter how long it takes.

The other day, Keith found his high school algebra textbook. Susan had no idea where he stored it in their decade together, but he saved the book since the Wheat Ridge days.

"I used to know how to do this," he told her. "Maybe I can again."

He tried, Susan said, to write out a few equations. His focus, squinting a few inches above paper, was absolute. He solved a few.

What must that be like, to lose so much? It's a lot like this, falling, getting up. Falling. Why the hell doesn't he pack it in?

Moving again, Keith shuffles to a bump in the trail. He stops, stares ahead. With his crooked helmet and the posture of a person cut adrift, from a distance he resembles a child with cerebral palsy.

Jon marveled at and was attracted to Keith's abilities — his intellect, his strength, his passion. How many times he trailed behind, admiringly, resentfully, competitively. So much changed in that Yakutat moment. Martin said Keith became an old man in one day. He lost more than most will ever have.

But he's still teaching, Jon thinks. *Pay attention.*

The messages are new for those of us accustomed to the ways of youthful exuberance. More subtle, maybe more important, certainly more profound: how do you look irretrievable loss in the face and keep on trying? Not the heroic loss of a friend who forgot to clip in before rappelling.

Tough to watch the bruising, but imagine living it day by day. Jon sees his friend cry, grieve. But Keith keeps on trying, continues to wrest a smile out of the simplest triumph.

On the snow hump, Keith leans forward and pushes on his poles. He jerks forward and prepares to fall. But this time he catches himself with a jab. He shoots forward. He rides out the trough on his heels without falling. He comes to a stop as the trail ramps upward.

"Yes!" he says, smiling back at Jon. A drop falls from his nose. Jon follows, skiing past a crimson dot on the snow.

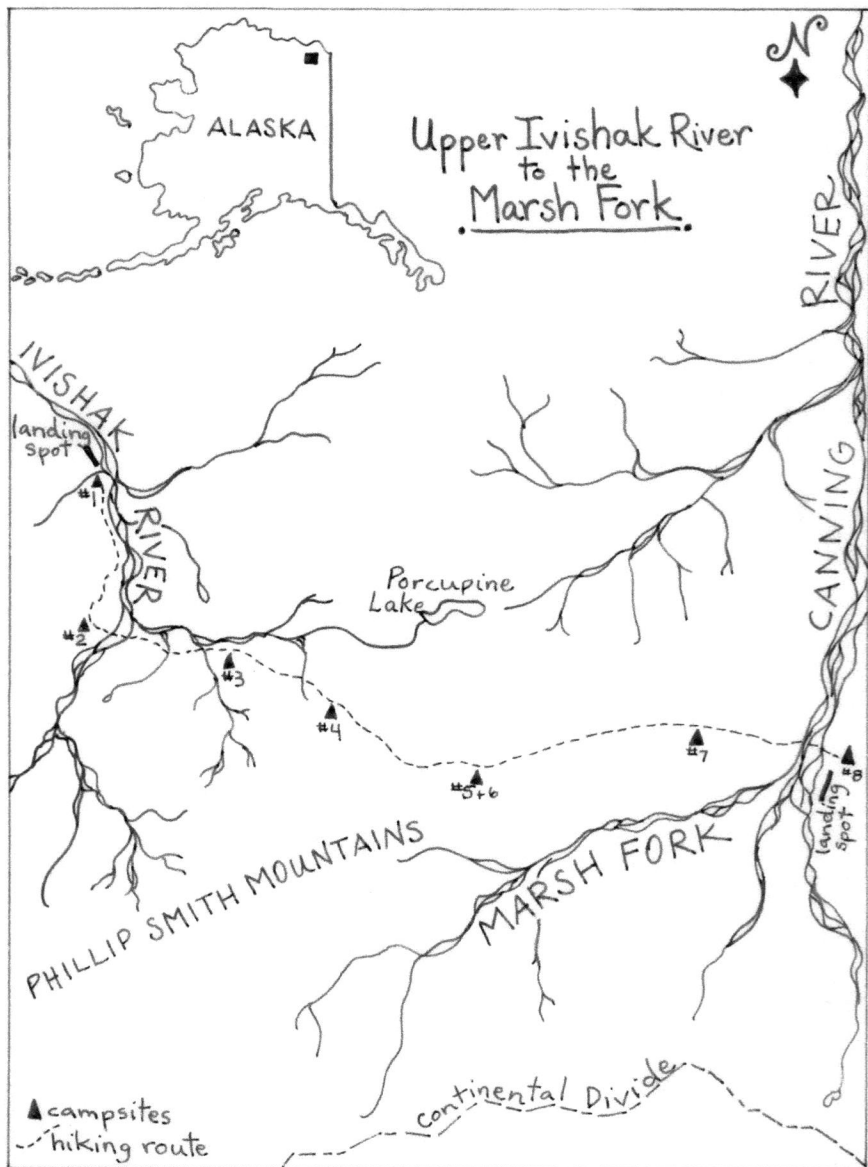

ALASKA

Upper Ivishak River
to the
Marsh Fork

N

IVISHAK

landing
spot

#1

RIVER

#2

#3

#4

Porcupine
Lake

#7

#8

#5+6

landing
spot

CANNING

RIVER

PHILLIP SMITH MOUNTAINS

MARSH FORK

▲ campsites
---- hiking route

continental Divide

14 | 7 years

Seven years to the day since Yakutat. A braided stream knocked small rocks along beneath its gray surface. The waterway was one of many Keith and Susan needed to cross on a 12-day hiking trip. The water did not seem like much of an obstacle.

This summer journey was almost like before. A walk in the Brooks Range, from the upper Ivishak River to the Marsh Fork of the Canning River. With five other friends.

The doctors were supportive of the venture, unusual for a brain-tumor patient. When Susan proposed a backpacking trip beyond the abilities of most of America's population, the doctors nodded. In Susan they saw a partner who knew what to do during seizures, who would make sure he took his medications, who would not freak out when the weird times happened.

Dr. David Reardon at Duke University's Preston Robert Tisch Brain Tumor Center was the first to give the backpacking trip a green light: *Heck yes. If you think you can do it, go.*

Backing up: Right after Yakutat and the diagnosis in Anchorage, Keith and Susan had flown to cancer centers in

Seattle, then San Francisco, looking for the treatment option that was right. They found it on the other side of the country, at Duke.

"I can fix that," a doctor said after shaking Keith's trembling hand, minutes after he arrived at the Duke examination room. The doctor stopped the tremor, by changing a medication and eliminating the side effect.

Soon after that introduction, Susan and Keith met David Reardon. In his office at Duke, they saw a solid man with a crewcut of salt and pepper. He was calm and professional, a relaxed speaker. His peers volunteered him to appear in front of cameras on telethons and other fundraisers. He always said yes.

Keith and Susan noticed a lack of ego that was not evident in some other people they met who operated on people's brains. Reardon stopped talking shortly after introducing himself. *Now tell me your story.*

Reardon seemed intrigued to meet someone who flew glaciers for a living. He prodded Keith for details on his plane, the laser-rangefinding system and flying in Alaska.

While Keith talked, Reardon looked over at a man with a red bandanna wrapped around his head. Radiation treatments had caused Keith to lose clumps of his dirty-blond hair. Listening to Keith's scratchy, soft voice, the doctor heard power. He envisioned Keith swinging his ice-axe into a quiet mountain wall, never thinking of falling. Expecting to make it to the top.

He looked to Susan, her right hand wrapped around Keith's left. He knew what the psychological evaluators would say: They probably wouldn't make it. A tumor puts so much strain on a relationship. A patient under treatment becomes a different person. Angry, bloated, not the person you signed up for. If you are not committed with every molecule, it will happen to you.

But right away, he sensed their rare connection. Her hazel eyes never left his as he explained their treatment options. He was a bit surprised as Keith pulled out a yellow notepad. In his terrible handwriting, he had written out questions for Dr. Reardon. Susan laughed when she struggled to read them out loud.

"Keith always stood out to me," said Reardon, who has seen more than 20,000 people with brain cancer in the last 20 years. "It was always a pleasure to see him. He had a way of making other people feel good."

Dr. Reardon knew that most with Keith's type of tumor die within a few years. He was soon to learn that Keith was one of a small subset on the right side of the bell curve.

For some reason, he responded well to treatments. Two years after his seizures at Yakutat, his tumor stalled.

He stopped oral chemotherapy and radiation. He regained the ability to walk long distances with a backpack. He remembered things, like mathematical equations and, a few times, how to solve them.

When Reardon saw Keith a year later, he was impressed at

how much outdoor activity Keith had been able to do. He then knew more about the capabilities of this stout patient from Alaska. He encouraged Keith and Susan to do anything they thought they could, with one caveat: that she was at his side.

Why are some patients able to live fuller lives than others? Dr. Reardon did not claim to know. But Keith's intention to beat cancer, and to enjoy what he could, probably made a difference.

"He never complained. That was a big factor in him. Not allowing circumstances to get the better of him and take over," Reardon said. "Many patients get pretty down and depressed. It's a tough road. But he had a remarkably inspirational attitude about it all. I think it helped."

Keith and Susan said yes to a wilderness hiking trip not long after an MRI showed a recurrence of the tumor a few years after he had stopped treatment. Its growth was aggressive, requiring him to resume chemotherapy and radiation.

They both thought he would be the one to beat the statistics, to slip past the death sentence on will and love and attitude. But, just like the first time, they did not let cancer take everything.

They gave the disease what it demanded: a week for radiation. Another for chemotherapy. But the other weeks were theirs. They would use two of them hiking in the Brooks Range.

Susan knew what the trip would demand of her. She was the one who knew to let the seizures run their course while removing objects from near his twitching body. She knew how wiped out he'd be after the shaking and would stay with him while the others moved ahead. She would wake in the tent, listening to him breathe, vigilant for any sign of a change.

She was part wife, part mother and a soul partner he could not do without. A delicate being who was the strongest he would ever meet in his years of clinging to cold mountains. Somehow, he had chosen just the right person.

Susan and Keith stood alone at the river crossing. Their friends had thought the knee-deep water was gentle enough. They had walked ahead after splashing through the river to the other side. They did not know what to expect of traveling with a cancer patient, but they remembered the Keith Echelmeyer of before and were mindful of not offering help until he asked.

"Ready?" Susan said.

Keith nodded. He had unbuckled the waist and chest straps of his backpack. It was standard procedure for river crossing, to allow for quick ditching if he should fall.

Before, he would find a heavy stick and hand it to Susan while crossing glacial rivers. He would enter the water with his boots on (to grip the cold rocks beneath) and his rainpants on (to keep his legs a bit warmer). He would face the current and stride out sideways, as if edging out on a plank. The cloudy glacial water hid the rocks, some of which he could feel bumping off his feet and shins. He would hold out the stick to her. She grabbed it and tried to walk in the eddy he created.

Sometimes, when the current was boiling, Keith would

stride over carrying both his pack and hers. He would drop them on the far bank of gravel. He would sway back to her through the water, a splashy weave that reminded her of a wooly mammoth.

"Are you ready?" he would ask her.

"A bit embarrassed, but yes," she said.

He then bent down so she could fold at the waist over his right shoulder. He straightened and turned with Susan's legs twirling the air. The fireman's carry.

"Believe it or not, it's easier this way," he said as if he was carrying nothing. "With you, the water doesn't push me around."

He would slosh her across and gently bend. He lowered her until her feet touched gravel. Then they shouldered their packs and resume hiking.

In this new reality, Susan was the lead. She squinted at the river, trying to remember the invisible lines where the others had crossed.

She chose. They stepped into the flow wearing their hiking boots. They both felt the breathless cold of water trickling into their boots, soaking their socks.

There were no sticks to be found. They locked arms; her right and his left.

After two halting steps, Keith leaned hard into her. She lost her balance, but did not fall.

He was wobbly as a moose calf, a chaotic motion Susan could not predict nor counter. He was simply too big for her to muscle. She told him something she never had.

"We can't do this. Let's get back to where we started."

She shuffled back to the dry gravel. He struggled to follow, as if his legs weren't obeying. The river had numbed his toes and feet. He swung his legs from the hip, clumsy.

They stood on the bank, dripping.

"I – I'm sorry," she said. "I just didn't think we were safe."

From Susan's Rite in the Rain Journal No. 391, Ivishak to the Marsh Fork.

I knew it was the right thing to do. I could not have held Keith up if he fell.

Our life before his brain tumor collided with the present moment. Loss and grieving washed over us.

After 30 minutes had passed, their friends returned to the river crossing. They saw Keith and Susan, still on the far side.

Stan Justice and Frank Keim splashed into the river without their packs. With few words, they walked Keith back into the water. Justice, a friend since their childhood days in Denver, held his right arm and Keim, a like-minded bird watcher and environmentalist, his left.

When Keith was across, Justice returned for Keith's backpack. He took Susan's arm and she crossed with him.

After thanking their friends, Keith and Susan said they would catch up with them soon. They needed a bit more time.

We walked upstream, away from the others, and cried. I tried to reassure him. What else could I do? We were all safe on this side. A golden eagle flew overhead.

Susan and Keith did not linger on the river crossing. They mourned what they had lost and were done with it. They thought of what they might write in their Book of Good Stuff that evening. The strength of friends was at the top of the list.

As the days passed and their bodies underwent the familiar acclimation to life in the mountains, they fed on the pleasant rhythm of walking uneven ground, and sleeping on tundra in their small North Face tent. They were getting what they came for.

Keith carried his 45-pound pack through shin-high tundra tussocks. Climbing through a high pass, he and Susan approached within five feet of a rosy finch feeding on a vole's stash of plant seeds. Caribou trails scratched high across the talus slopes. They imagined those royal creatures, noses in the air as they carried velveted racks that grew inches every summer day.

One step at a time, they made it to campsites chosen by their friends each arctic evening. They laughed, shared boiled meals and observations of the day. It felt like any other trip. At times, Keith's friends forgot he was sick.

On the 12th day, they wound between dagger limestone peaks to the arranged pick-up point, a wide gravel bar on the Canning River. Two weeks through the heart of a great wilderness, no trails. Carrying all their food and their room for the night. Rain and mosquitoes and sunshine and the glory and uncertainty of silent, raw country.

A chemotherapy appointment the next day was far from Keith's thoughts there on the gravel of the Canning River. He had returned to the country that was so much a part of him: The Brooks Range, his favorite place in this land he knew so well. Drinking its clear waters and sleeping on its cushion of hardy plants. It was a tonic his spirit needed ever since his first climbing trip to Alaska in the van with his buddies.

We were so fortunate to be able to do this with friends. For so long, I thought we'd never backpack in the Brooks Range again.

He was at home.

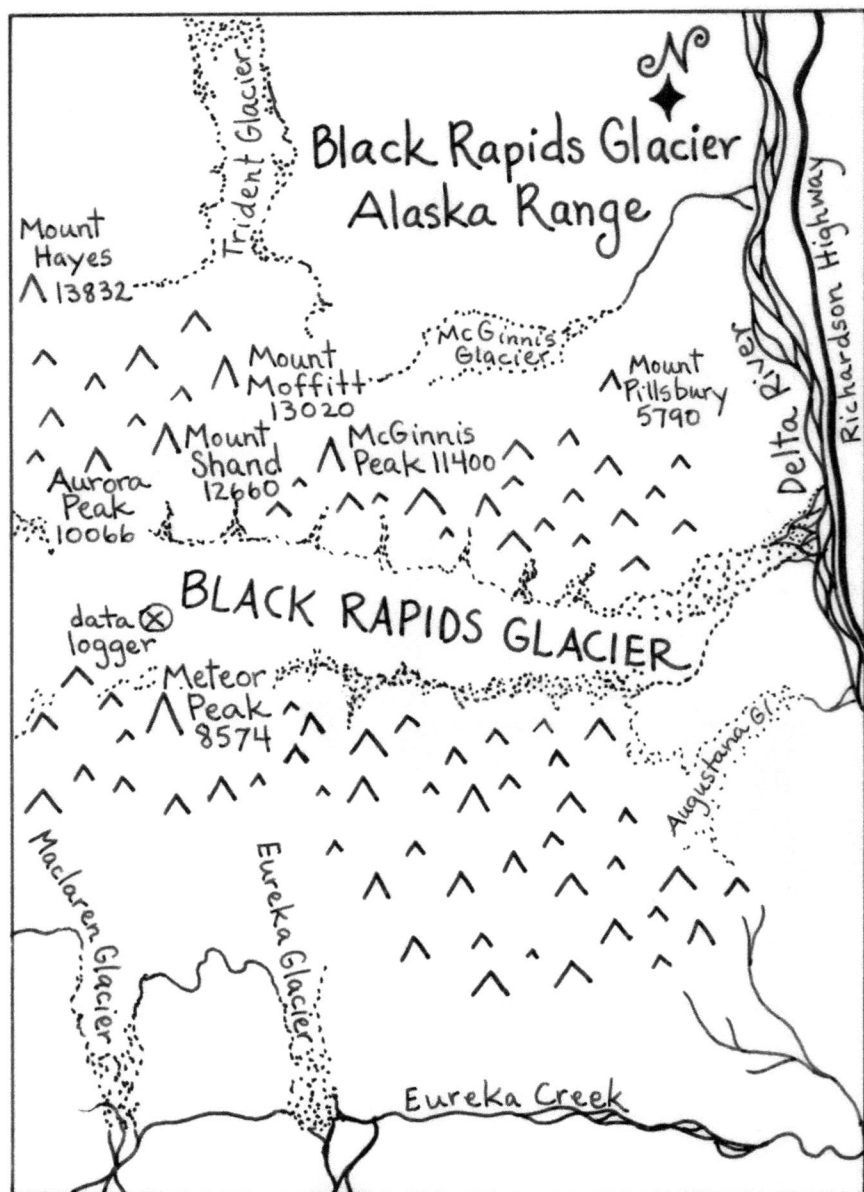

Black Rapids Glacier
Alaska Range

Trident Glacier

Mount Hayes
⋀ 13832

McGinnis Glacier

Mount Pillsbury
5790

⋀ Mount Moffitt
13020

⋀ Mount Shand
12660

⋀ McGinnis Peak 11400

Aurora Peak
10066

Delta River

Richardson Highway

data logger ⊗

BLACK RAPIDS GLACIER

⋀ Meteor Peak
8574

Augustana Gl.

Maclaren Glacier

Eureka Glacier

Eureka Creek

15 | Last trip to Black Rapids

Is that you, Rich?

Keith spoke over his aircraft radio to a blinking plane, flying in the dark over Black Rapids Glacier. There, Keith had landed on skis in the dark heart of winter.

Just after he touched down, in the muted blue light of January, Keith felt a sickening drop. *Whump.* The Piper's skis had sunk into waist-deep snow.

As Keith gunned the engine, the plane's nose and propeller nodded toward the snow. He backed off the throttle and said a bad word.

Stuck. His backseat passenger and helper for the day, Kent Swanson, felt an iceball form in his gut. The temperature in Fairbanks had been 12 below zero. It was minus 25 on the glacier.

Rich Flanders, a fellow owner of a Piper PA-12, had met Keith on the Juneau Icefield in 1974. After they both followed adventurous paths and lost touch, almost 20 years later they found out they were neighbors in Fairbanks.

Their twin aircraft and shared interests inspired many boyish times in a sky, with few restrictions: dogfighting their small planes as they banked over the spruce curves of Wood River. Flying in formation with Bob Hammond in his Cessna 140 beneath the Yukon River Bridge: three small planes flying side by side between concrete support towers, the outer two flaring like swallows on the far side.

In their small subset of the fraternity of Fairbanks bush pilots, Flanders, Keith and a few others were on alert to help one another avoid embarrassing and sometimes costly official rescues. Like the January day Susan called Flanders.

"Where does Keith usually park his plane?" she asked.

"Why do you want to know?" Flanders said.

He was two hours overdue on his flight plan, Susan said. Someone from the FAA called and wanted to know where he might have landed in town, if he had made it that far.

"I know where he probably is," Flanders said. "I'll call the center and tell them to hold off until I check it out."

What was he doing down there in January, when the sun rose at 10 a.m. and was gone before 3?

Flanders had a hunch Keith was doing a flyover of his equipment and had landed for some reason. He knew Keith had deployed 35-millimeter cameras at various points along the glacier to get a time-lapse of glacier motion.

Flanders glanced out his window. His neighbor, also a pilot, happened to be driving home.

Chris Puchner said yes, he had just landed his Cessna 180. Sure, he'd be willing to go back up while the engine was warm and do a flyover of Black Rapids.

As he pulled on his flight gear, Flanders somehow knew Keith was OK. Puchner and Flanders flew down to the glacier the quick way, passing between the massifs of Deborah and Hess. Puchner banked left when he reached the high ice divide, and started down Black Rapids. An hour before, the sun had dropped behind Denali to the southwest.

Keith and Swanson heard the echo of the engine long before they saw a blinking strobe. They could not see the shape of the plane in the dark, but Keith thought one of his imagined scenarios might be playing out.

"Is that you, Rich?" Keith called over his VHF radio.

Flanders smiled and keyed the mic of Puchner's radio.

"Yup. What's your story?"

"My Rossignols aren't much good for packing a runway."

"Someday I'm gonna hide a pair of snowshoes in your plane," Flanders said. Puchner circled his plane high, at 9,000 feet, about 500 feet higher than nearby Meteor Peak.

"Listen, I'll fly back tomorrow a little after daybreak. I'll bring the Red Dragon and a pair of shoes. You guys got what you need for an overnight?"

"Yeah, sleeping bags and a bit of food. Thanks."

Puchner dialed in a new frequency and called the control

tower at Fairbanks. He asked a controller there to relay a message to the Rescue Control Center at an Air Force base in Anchorage. Puchner told them the plane's position and that there was no need for a rescue helicopter.

The next day, January 13, was cold and clear. In his PA-12, Flanders touched his skis down on the downhill slope of the glacier, dragged two lines in the snow and then lifted off again. He looped back, heading upglacier, and landed smack on his ski lines. He then taxied at full power, pivoted around on the snow and ferried back to his ski marks.

Puchner, who had flown down again, circled overhead, staying in radio contact.

As Swanson stomped out an airstrip with the snowshoes, happy at the movement and warmth, Flanders pulled out his Red Dragon propane heater. Keith dragged it across the snow to his plane. Flanders fired it up, then pulled off his gloves. The 25 below air stung his fingers until he held them in the flow of hot air from the duct Keith was pointing at his engine. Their goal was to warm the oil without setting the Piper on fire.

In a few hours, they were all back in Fairbanks.

Over the years, the broad canyon of Black Rapids echoed with a few pilot errors. Keith once pancaked his landing gear into the glacier while landing in fog on a slope that was steeper than it looked.

"He was a very proficient pilot," Flanders said of his friend. "But sometimes he had a judgment problem."

Close calls and walk-away crashes did not deter Keith. He

executed more than 100 landings on what was to become his most familiar face of ice.

Named for a vigorous section of the Delta River, Black Rapids flows the length of a running marathon from about its beginnings at an ice divide it shares at 6,000 feet with Susitna Glacier.

The glacier is more than 2,000 feet thick in its upper reaches as it pours from the higher peaks of the eastern Alaska Range to the lowlands of the Interior. Just to the north are Aurora Peak (10,000 feet), and Mount Shand (12,660), Mount Moffit (13,020) and McGinnis Peak (11,400).

The Delta River takes Black Rapids' considerable outflow and freights its load of ground-up mountain to the swamps of middle Alaska. With the help of big winds, some glacial flour deposited on islands has constructed the hills of the Tanana River uplands. Some powder in concentrate makes it to the Yukon River, all the way to the Bering Sea.

When Alaska was a young state, Black Rapids earned a nickname, the Galloping Glacier. In the late 1930s, people at the Black Rapids Roadhouse sent a radio message to Fairbanks. The roadhouse was on the Richardson Highway, a muddy trail from Valdez to Fairbanks that evolved into one of the state's first highways.

Glacier is heading toward us. Sounds of thunder and huge chunks that look closer every day. Has moved more than one mile our direction in a month.

Bradford Washburn, mountaineer and director of the

Boston Museum of Science, called the report "absolute hokum."

Jim Hance was the first scientist to take a look. He pounded in stakes at the crumbling ice face. The glacier's tongue advanced three miles from September 1936 to February 1937. It was moving an average distance of 115 feet each day.

Other scientists, including University of Alaska Museum collector Otto Geist, traveled down to witness the scene. As he measured, he wondered if the glacier might dam the Delta River with its ice blocks. Ancient moraines showed Black Rapids had done just that more than once, resulting in a giant lake being formed in the low pass now used by highway travelers.

Geist made hourly measurements in April 1937, which turned out to be the end of the gallop. Just as quickly as Black Rapids had started, it stopped.

Black Rapids was surging, one of a handful in Alaska that suddenly spilled forward after years of gaining quiet weight in its upper reaches. Scientists had postulated that unusual snow years or jolts from earthquakes may be the reason glaciers surge. But those ideas did not pass muster. Black Rapids and other surging glaciers did not react that way to a 7.9 earthquake, and others took off regardless of how much snow they received in accumulation areas up high.

Why a glacier surges was a nice, clean problem to study. One that involved hot-water drills to make holes to the base of a glacier where ice slides along bedrock. And survey stakes, ice-penetrating radar and laser altimetry from a small plane.

The glacier was everything a flyer wanted. Its upper basins,

Trinity and Loket, are wide and smooth, almost flat to their divides. The flight from Fairbanks is just over one hour. The approaches between peaks were more than one mile wide. In good weather, "you can land with your eyes closed," Flanders says. Takeoffs are a gravity-assisted slide with an easy escape over the Delta River. Across the highway was an airstrip Keith used for ferrying gear and people.

Unlike most Alaska glaciers, this one had literature. Austin Post, the Ansel Adams of glacier photography, had written of the Black Rapids surge. In part by analyzing the loops of moraine on the upper glacier left behind by previous advances, Larry Mayo constructed a history of the glacier's behavior for those concerned it might someday overtake the proposed oil pipeline. He and Post mapped the shore of an ancient lake that formed when the glacier once stopped up the river. Mayo concluded that Black Rapids had last charged forward during the term of George Washington.

Will Harrison spent so much time up high that two of the monuments cemented in for Black Rapids geodetic surveys are named for him. "Will's ear" is just north of "Will's left ear."

Will introduced Keith to the glacier shortly after Keith arrived in Alaska, right as USGS funding was waning. Each spring, the glacier was a destination for Keith and the graduate students who worked with him. Everyone in the Glaciers Lab was involved, but the body of ice flowing along the Denali Fault became Keith's baby.

When he could not do summer-long campaigns on Black Rapids, Keith would fly up on his way to other places. He would land, dig out stakes or place a few time-lapse cameras.

One of the recurring tasks was to monitor and maintain a simple set of metal poles stuck in the glacier. The 10-foot sections of inch-diameter electrical conduit run down the upper basins, each one about six miles apart. Frozen in with a backpack-mounted hot-water hose, the poles tell a glaciologist 1) how much snow has fallen up high the previous winter and 2) how much the glacier has oozed downhill in a year.

Each spring, Keith landed high on the glacier to find the posts. He would measure how much snow had fallen and — when snowfall was great — clamp another section of pipe to a buried one. When glacier movement required it, he would drive another pipe in its upper reaches.

Keith executed this duty in early April, when glacier time, in stable weather, is sunny and warm enough to sometimes work without mittens.

Martin Truffer was the scientist to whom Keith would hand Black Rapids. It became somewhat official on a perfect spring day, a few years after Martin's daughter Sonja became the first baby Keith ever held.

April 5, 2009, was a pilot's dream: Cold still air beneath a robin-egg sky. Sunshine sharpening every crack. The promise of 13 hours of light on the glacier.

Yakutat had been seven years ago. In days he earned with sheer will, Keith battled to get things back. Walking. Skiing. Remembering the range of the bristle-thighed curlew and the Latin name of the twinflower. He could not fly, but his friends could.

Four pilots landed single-engine planes on the ice that day. Martin Truffer and Martin Stueffer in the PA-12 Stueffer had purchased from Keith. Chris Larsen in a Cessna 140. Rich Flanders in his PA-12. Noticing her friends were there, Kristin Nolan landed in her Super Cub.

Keith flew to Black Rapids with Flanders. They took off from a private airstrip on a hill above a Fairbanks subdivision.

Flanders and Keith floated over Tanana Flats. Moose seeking shade from the early April sun dropped to the snow and bedded down. The friends topped the backbone of Iowa Ridge and climbed to 10,000 feet. They were soon on a magic carpet between familiar blue-white peaks. Keith could see rocky shelves upon which he had rested during climbs.

Over Black Rapids, Flanders made his uphill approach and felt a stiffness to his skis as he dragged them. The snow was firm.

Upon landing on the glacier, Keith's face crinkled into a smile. Flanders taxied next to Truffer's wingtip and cut the engine. Silence washed over the basin.

The four planes on the glacier were the most Keith had seen in this place, a world of ice and rock he knew as well as his childhood bedroom on Newland Street.

Keith wore bunny boots, blue climbing pants with pile patches on the knees and a balaclava. He was happy to feel the 10-degree chill, especially on the half of his body facing away from the sun. He stood on the platform of snow for a second, feeling like someone visiting his hometown after years away, wondering if he would ever get back.

His friends and colleagues converged on him carrying pipes, tools, and the backpack-mounted water heater. They all wore dark sunglasses and smiles, knowing they had hit the weather.

"Let's get to work," Keith said. "There's a post not too far from here."

The labor was relaxed but efficient, as everyone knew they would fly their machines back before the late subarctic nightfall.

And they worked. Keith was soon to learn of a second tumor in his brain, one that would end his life. But that day, he was there to lead almost as he once did. He took his turn clamping on new conduit extensions and instructing Martin how best to work the hot-water drill.

The air was crisp and smelled of melted snow, a scent that said spring, hope and energy. As was his learned habit, Keith savored every second of working with his people. In his place, again. He looked up and imagined ruby-crowned kinglets returning from Mexico to flood the forest with song.

Over lunch and hot tea from a thermos, Flanders pulled off his sunglasses and cleaned them with his shirttail. He squinted at the black face of McGinnis Peak. Its southern couloir, a steep gash in the mountain, was one of the most difficult routes in Alaska.

"You and Jon tried to climb that, right?" Flanders said.

"Yeah, we got about right there," Keith said, pointing with a wedge of pilot bread. "Had to get back down when it got warm and started raining rocks."

He smiled. Everyone smiled. And, for a few seconds, no one spoke. The ice hissed with quiet in the icy palm between the fingers of Shand, Aurora, Moffit and McGinnis.

Though everyone thought about finality during those eight hours on the glacier, no one talked about it. Everyone instead looked around at mountain walls, snowshoe tracks leading to work accomplished and the flying machines ready to take them home.

.

ALASKA

Keith's Last Camp
Arctic National Wildlife Refuge
Brooks Range

N

mountains

— dryas bench–
Super cub
landing spot

ℇ₃m

willows

Keith
+
Susan

Cane Creek

Laurie

fire

gravel
bar

willows

1m high
bench

Jen
+
Frank

Stan

X Keith's
napping
spot–
waiting
for the plane

willows

X
bear
stood up,
sniffed

↙bear

mountains
in the distance

(Drawn from a
sketch in Keith
and Susan's last
trip journal
June 7, 2010)

16 | 8 years

Flying to Arctic Village from his base in Fort Yukon, Kirk Sweetsir wondered what form of Keith Echelmeyer he would see at the village airstrip.

One year earlier, Sweetsir had picked up Keith, Susan and their friends on the Canning River after two weeks of summer hiking.

On this day, Sweetsir was flying his blue and white Cessna 185 to Arctic Village. He would land there to ferry Keith to the Arctic National Wildlife Refuge for another backpacking trip. The plan: Six friends, 11 days. Backpack from Cane Creek over the Continental Divide and the spine of the Brooks Range to the Marsh Fork of the Canning River.

Sweetsir bounced to a landing in Arctic Village, a small community of a few hundred Gwichin Natives well north of the Arctic Circle. More than 75 miles from Venetie, Arctic Village is one of the most isolated settlements on the continent.

As Sweetsir taxied, he saw Keith, a bit hunched, but still Keith. His propeller stopped spinning and Keith, Susan and their four friends approached.

Keith strode over with the help of hiking poles. They hung from his wrists as he embraced Sweetsir with a hug that was surprising in its firmness.

"You ready to go?" Sweetsir said.

"Let's get her packed," Keith said. He was beaming from under the visor of a baseball cap.

Like few others, Sweetsir knew how Keith needed the quiet forest of black and white spruce, the whisper of nameless creeks, the ptarmigan chicks scooting between the alpine rocks, invisible except for their movement.

He watched Keith now as he shuffled with his backpack toward the plane. For the first time, he wondered if this person was fit for a 100-mile traverse through the wilderness.

He looked at Susan, who smiled back with her dimples and youthful enthusiasm. He glanced back at Keith, who had an arm on his plane door and seemed to be resting. Sweetsir's analysis was then complete: No one — not Keith nor Susan nor their friends nor any doctor — knew what to expect out there. But they were going to try.

He flew the party to a natural bench of ankle-high vegetation about one-half hour north of Arctic Village. They were at the foot of a mountain that seemed to be stripped clean of vegetation, leaving a slope of gray/green rocks.

After landing, he helped Keith, Stan Justice and Susan extract their backpacks. He hugged Keith again and had a few words for Susan.

"If you need me, use that sat-phone. I'll be flying some other parties into ANWR the next few days and might be around."

She smiled and nodded.

Sweetsir's plane buzzed painful echoes off the mountain. The forever silence returned to this unpeopled corner of Alaska.

"I love that sound," Keith said.

"You mean the lack of sound?" Justice asked.

"Yeah."

They camped on a flat of dryas flowers, which resembled a meeting hall of nodding, white-haired professors. A creek gurgled just steps away. A gravel pad nearby was a nice place for a campfire.

Justice gathered dead willow sticks while Susan and Keith set up their tent. The other travelers — Frank and Jennifer Keim and Laurie Leonard — found flat spots for their tents.

There was a slight breeze to shove the mosquitoes. No clouds. Temperature in the high 60s, just about perfect. Mountains surrounded them. When they squinted, they saw the snowy pinpoints of Dall sheep. Blooming wildflowers perfumed the air. Robins sang from willow branches.

They camped in the same spot for two nights. They had the time, and it was too beautiful to hike away.

On the second day, they walked around to explore the

landscape. It would also test their capabilities.

Keith stumbled through tussock tundra. The footing was chaotic — shin-high mushroom heads with puddles in between — but he had been able to negotiate similar terrain the year before.

During the last 12 months, doctors had discovered a second brain tumor. It was growing, as was the first. Treatments had little effect.

Keith was losing the abilities he had fought so hard for. Concentration was a problem. Why was he holding his toothbrush? He often fell to the ground; trekking poles were a necessity, even for checking the mailbox.

On the tundra, Keith called out to Susan.

"Can you help? My feet aren't moving right."

Susan felt a white chill as she hiked over to him. With his left arm around her shoulder, she helped him back to their campsite. He fell into the tent and onto his sleeping bag. She covered him with her bag. He was soon snoring.

Susan pulled out her Rite in the Rain All-Weather Line Rule, Notebook No. 391: Cane Creek — Marsh Fork:

Something is happening.

Having watched from afar, their friends knew: Keith would not be hiking with them across the divide. He would not be walking anywhere.

And they could not help but listen as, after dinner, Susan

pulled out the satellite phone and dialed the number for Kirk Sweetsir. She caught the pilot right before he was headed out for the day. Yes, he said, he could land in exactly the same spot tomorrow afternoon. He could fly Keith and Susan back to Fort Yukon. From there, they could catch the afternoon commercial flight back to Fairbanks.

Susan walked back to their gathering circle near the creek. She told her friends what they already knew.

"You guys should get going tomorrow morning," she said. "You'll need that time so your days near the end aren't too long."

"Nope, we're staying until you guys leave," Justice said.

"No discussion," Frank Keim said.

"We'll do a day hike today so you and Keith can have some time together," Justice said. "Just head over that ridge and see what's there. We'll be back in the afternoon."

Susan nodded.

Keith slept in the tent after breakfast. Even if the decision not to proceed was heartbreaking, at least it was a clear call.

Justice, Leonard and the Keims walked a short distance up a hill to a waterfall and vanished. Susan was surprised when they returned just 30 minutes later.

"A grizzly is headed this way," Frank Keim said. "It's moving toward us. Should be able to see it soon if it hasn't changed course."

Suddenly, there it was. Traipsing across the tundra, sniffing the invisible path the hikers had just laid.

Its back was glistening, blonde with a dark stripe down the spine. Its gait was heavy, pounding the moss.

The grizzly squinted toward their tents and campfire coals and altered its course, arcing in a wide curve around them. It wanted nothing to do with these people in its country, but it didn't seem scared.

A word came to Susan's poet mind: Wild. She remembered it when it was time to write in her journal.

Day 4: Exactly 8 years ago today, Keith was medivacked from Yakutat to Anchorage. Eight years.

Sitting here, on this sunny dryas bench, our friends already upriver and out of sight, headed to the Marsh Fork, it seems like a cruel trick. Our packs are packed, Keith is curled on the tundra asleep. We're waiting for Kirk to come pick us up. Keith's right leg and arm are worse. He's having trouble finding his thoughts. We're entering new territory. How cruel will it be?

Keith woke with a start. Susan thought he might be having a seizure. He gathered himself just enough to say what he'd been thinking. He looked into Susan's eyes.

"You can just leave me out here," he said. "I want it this way."

Part of Susan, her heart, thought that made perfect sense. Keith fading in his beloved Brooks Range. Ravens would be first to start his transformation to earth. His DNA running through beetles, voles and foxes. He would be happy with that.

The other part of her, the side brought up as a little girl in Wisconsin, knew it was not to be.

She did not know what to do. They both knew they would someday reach this distant valley. There was no map.

Keith's unusual strength and will and the love of Susan and their friends and family had pushed that misty terrain miles into the future. But here it was: Treeless hills, a clear stream, wind through willow leaves, the smell of sedge, the indifferent whine of mosquitoes.

We still name "good things" about each day and Keith doesn't want to dwell on "this," but it's impossible to avoid this feeling of dread, a shadow creeping onto the landscape of this life we have been tenderly transforming. What will happen next? How will we bear it?

While she was writing, they heard the distant roar of Sweetsir's plane. They had, as if underwater, helped one another roll the North Face tent. They both wondered if it was the last time they had slept in it together.

Sweetsir's plane stopped rolling. The air was silent for a second before the door of his plane creaked open.

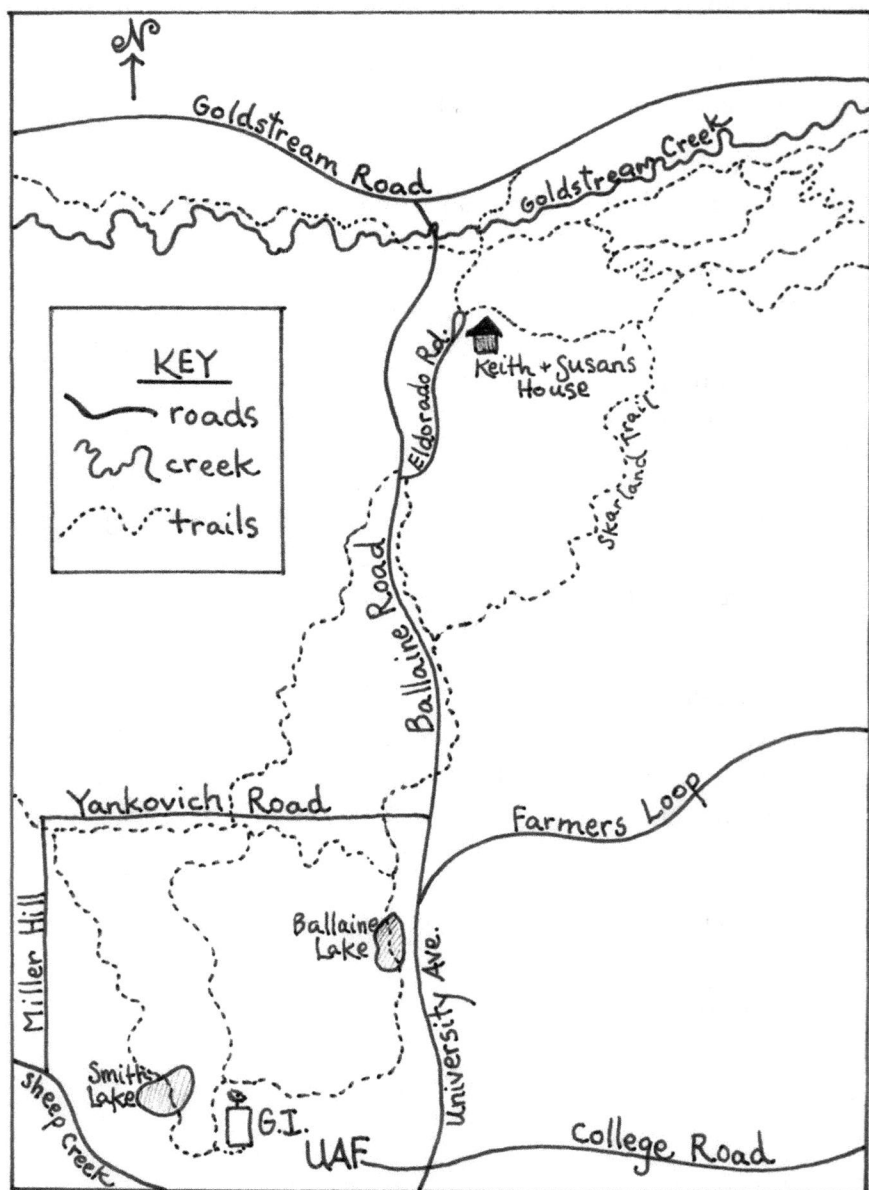

17 | Eldorado Road

It was time for me to visit the home of Keith and Susan. He had stopped eating and drinking. There was not much time left.

Over the years, I held different feelings toward Keith Echelmeyer. Before his brain tumor, I was a bit intimidated.

I was the runner who trained all summer for the marathon; he was the guy who passed me going up Ester Dome after a season of flying and climbing mountains. I was the guy who ate my toothpaste and bled through my boots during the wilderness race. He was the one who won it in half the time it took me. He was the dashing glacier pilot and scientist who designed studies and wrote complex papers and did first ascents.

He was the hardass academic and field advisor to my graduate student friends. They were young studs funhogging their way through Alaska for a few years while earning a degree. They could not match his intellect, nor endure cold as well as Keith, nor carry as much on their backs. And he let them know it.

I related better to his students, like Adam Bucki, with

whom I shared an office when my supervisor found room for me in the Glaciers Lab. Adam and I skied together and went on a caribou hunt and ran an ultramarathon together on Kodiak Island. Most everything Keith did seemed beyond my skills.

After his brain tumor, I would see the newly retired Keith once in a while in the halls of the Geophysical Institute building. He was always walking with Susan. I would try not to register my surprise at his swollen face or his stooped posture.

But my reaction did not matter. He always had a smile and opened his arms for a hug. That hit me in the heart every time. Who is this new guy? And how can he be so happy after losing so much?

We always paused for a chat, one time about the bird class he was taking and how his ability to remember their Latin names was improving. He lingered, asking about my wife and little girl, something he might not have done before. Time and deadlines no longer seemed to matter.

And standing there, always, was Susan.

Late in September 2010, I was feeling sorry for myself in my temporary gig as a single parent. My daughter Anna was 4 at the time. My wife Kristen was somewhere in the wilds of Alaska, studying birds. I had little time for anything but daddying, writing my column and getting the dog out for a walk.

I started reading Susan's entries on a website called Caring Bridge. Perhaps the best use so far of the Internet, the site allows loved ones to post updates on people who are dying or otherwise having a rough go. It's newsy for friends and relatives and cathartic for the person doing the writing.

Links would appear in my inbox after she had written a new entry on Keith. I read them right away, and went back to re-read them several times during the day.

After showing him a picture of Denali and watching his finger run down Cassin Ridge, she asked if he missed the mountain:

His expression changes, becomes wistful, he nods yes.

I feel as though my heart will break open with the sudden sense of longing and loss, tears roll down my cheeks. I wonder how he can bear this, bear being unable to walk or even move on his own after a lifetime of skiing, hiking and climbing.

Keith looks at me with clear eyes, still smiling, with an enigmatic expression that I can only interpret to mean: "It's still here, it's all still inside me. The sunlight and shadow of hundreds of mountains. Stone, talus and snow. Wildflowers and wild creatures, the breath and scent of every peak and escarpment, every approach and ascent. Every cold night, every clear morning. Every descent. All the long days waiting for weather. Each route unfolding, unfolding, unfolding. The inexhaustible adventure and beauty."

There was something special going on at the end of Eldorado Drive. I had to go see it.

What did I expect? I didn't know. Susan hinted that Keith was seeing things on his deathbed that his visitors could not. She wrote of a spiritual connection with the world even when he was bed-bound. A tether to some special place that got stronger the closer he got to dying.

With his brainpower, Keith could have been a great theoretical physicist, solving incomprehensible, important problems and sharing the results in lecture halls.

But he had to be a field scientist to see the heart of the world. He craved the fuzzy natural connections he could never explain. As Jon Miller said, a flock of white ptarmigan flushing in cold rosy light was as important to him as a well-climbed pitch. As Martin Truffer said, he needed to be out there in the mysteries of nature.

Driving to Eldorado Drive on that late September afternoon, I was scared. I could still turn around in those few miles and go home, avoid this difficult encounter. I almost stopped the car.

But soon I was parked by Keith's woodshed, unbuckling Anna from her car seat. She bolted toward the porch.

Susan greeted us both with a hug. She then swept up Anna. They were soon reading a book in the corner.

Anna noticed the man in the hospital bed by the window. She made her quiet assessment and turned toward Susan.

With my girl occupied and a hot mug of tea placed in my hands, I sat in a rocking chair. Keith was at the window, hands folded in front of him, breathing shallow breaths. He appeared to be sleeping.

Early that morning, just after midnight, Susan had spoon-fed him 24 ounces of slushy lemonade. *He was like a little bird, reaching his tongue for each bite.* But he had not responded to the spoon since.

All day, I've been trying hard to accept the fact that Keith may be finished drinking. Part of me knows that I can honor that, knows it is the right thing to do. At the same time, there is another part of me that is afraid. Afraid that I am not ready to let go of him. But how could I ever be ready, even after 8 years of moving toward this time? I am trying hard to let go of the things I think I should have figured out and just pay attention and be present for what is happening in each moment. A difficult thing to do, but I'm trying.

They had made an agreement. If she couldn't just leave him out in the middle of the Brooks Range, he wanted to die at home. No feeding him through tubes or intravenous hydration, or using any other mechanical means to prolong his life. When he could still talk, he asked her to promise him. She did.

My god, what a wonderful way to die. Not surrounded by beeping machines, antiseptic odors and strangers checking in every few hours until their shift ends. There was Keith, nodding toward the warm autumn light through the west windows. A few feet beyond, chickadees pulled sunflower seeds from a feeder.

During our visit, other friends of Keith's showed up. They found themselves with a mug of tea in their hands.

Each would go up to him, whisper a few words, gently touch his hands, kiss him on the cheek.

Then his friends — on that day all of them older than the 56-year-old Keith — told stories, like the one about flying together beneath the Yukon River Bridge. Laughter wafted up toward the ceiling. It was a party.

To Anna's delight, a woman arrived with her daughter, named Grace. Grace, about the same age as Anna, was still wearing her ballet outfit after practice. Soon, two girls were twirling on the rug in front of Keith. He did not seem to notice. Everyone else applauded. The girls bowed.

An hour later, I had to drag my girl out of there. As we walked down the steps, I looked back toward the living room. Through the windows, Keith's friends were doubled over, laughing at a story.

I left feeling happy. Didn't expect that. My mood was much lighter than the one I carried up the steps. We felt no gloom and doom (after all, wasn't death perched outside in a birch?) Nobody cried. No one asked why. Everybody laughed.

How did she do that?

Susan updated the journal just after midnight.

The poet, Denise Levertov, wrote: "Grief is a hole you walk around in the daytime and at night you fall into it."

There have been many times over the past 8 years that this has been true, but it is not true now.

Dear Friends, we feel your arms around us, holding us close, sheltering us from a chasm of grief. Even now, late at night, when only Keith and I are here, your presence is tangible, shining a rarified light on this mysterious landscape.

Two days later, Keith died at home. Six of his friends were in the room. At 6 in the evening, Susan was sitting next to him, holding him in her arms. The post-equinox sun was shining through a lace of clouds.

Susan noticed a sudden difference in his breathing. Each inhale was smooth, less of a struggle. The cadence slowed. Four seconds between breaths. Five. Ten.

Then stillness.
Stillness.
Peaceful stillness.
Such tender stillness.

Just before he died, he opened his eyes and looked at Susan. The right corner of his mouth curved up. He smiled.

You know he was seeing something we don't know.

Epilogue

I asked for health, that I might do great things.
I was given infirmity, that I might do better things.

Prayer of a Confederate Soldier

Martin Truffer: "The most amazing thing about his last 10 years of life is that he accepted. I'm never going to be the whiz kid. I'm never going to be the athlete. He became almost more inspirational when he wasn't doing amazing things."

Lore Johnson, Keith's childhood friend in Wheat Ridge: "I find it very interesting that his brain was the thing to shut down. It had to be that to get his heart to open. He still had the strength, but also a softness. He was more present. Would look at you longer in your eyes."

Anthony Arendt: "Before, he was a tough guy to get along with out there. He always wanted people to be at his level and he was frustrated when they weren't . . . On McCall Glacier, we hiked in once. All of a sudden three feet of snow fell. He was a little disappointed we couldn't keep up with him. We had a bag of brownies for the next three days. He ended up carrying everything and was still miles ahead of us.

After he got sick, he suddenly got transformed into a person who accepted all these weaknesses. He wasn't so black and white. A shade of gray started to emerge. He was OK if you weren't perfect with something."

Jon Miller: "Our friendship, as deep as it had once been, it got deeper. That that can come out of something so terrible is one of those few lessons in life that are profound and transformative. He had so much taken away from him, and he continued to powerfully, cheerfully persevere. He's an incredible role model for all the adversity we're going to face in life. Both he and Susan gave us a road map."

Roman Motyka: "(His sickness) could have crushed him but instead he went the other direction. Once he accepted it, he opened up his heart."

Richard Flanders: "He was arrogant to some degree but mostly he was impatient with people who didn't think they could do something. He just didn't think he had any limits. He was a driven person, and his sickness was another mountain to climb."

Will Harrison: "He gave the impression it was all one great adventure. And maybe it was."

A page from a "Good Stuff" Journal

March 18, 2005
- After 2 hard days of seizures + sadness, today was calm.
- Keith had better balance today.
- "I tied my own shoes!"
- Short walk on Goldstream Trail—
  - sunlight glinting on snow
  - hawk owl perched at top of a spruce
  - Walking! "Like hope shining in each step."
- Late afternoon—sitting by the woodstove warm!
- Patty (mom) called tonight—laughter filled the room
- Almut called from Germany. So good.
- A sliver of moon + a skyful of stars is shining tonight. Beauty breathes around us.

Thank you

to Brian Rogers and Mike Sfraga, for finding money to help me tell this story.

to the University of Alaska Foundation, for providing that money.

to Susan Morgan, editor and great encourager. She volunteered her reading and suggesting skills after reading that Keith and Susan's home became "a place of light" during his last days. She was faithful, affirming and necessary.

to Jessie Cherry, for intelligent readings and insight on what it's like to fly over Alaska.

to Andy Sterns, for helping me think like a climber and being my friend.

to Jon Miller, for soulful critique and allowing me to copy his own writing style in recalling his good friend and mountain partner.

to Patty Echelmeyer, for hosting me in Keith's boyhood home, for making me tuna sandwiches with chocolate milk, for taking me birding at Red Rocks before the Skrillex concert.

to Randy Sue and Ken Fosha, for teaching me square dancing, talking to me, and otherwise making me feel like Drowsy Water Ranch was home.

to Lore Johnson, for insight on a person she loved and understood.

to Rich Flanders, who knew what a friend he had.

to Kate Rogers for critique that made a difference.

to Rob McCue and Phil Marshall for thoughtful readings.

to Mark Adams for professional, instantaneous feedback.

to Martin Truffer, Chris Larsen, Will Harrison, Roman Motyka, Anthony Arendt, By Valentine, Adam Bucki, Shad O' Neel, Dan Elsberg, Patty Delvecchio, Craig Lingle, Gary Holton, John Power, Franz Mueter, Mike Ruckhaus and all of Keith's friends with brains large enough to also hang with him in a professional setting.

to Bob McCoy of the Geophysical Institute for patience and support of this work.

to Sue Mitchell for supporting this work with understanding and funding.

to Vicki Daniels for her artist's eye and talent.

to my girls, wife Kristen and daughter Anna, for keeping it light.

to Susan Campbell, for more than words can convey. Here's a try: Her kindness, compassion, coaching, sharing beyond reason, willingness to walk back along scary paths.

To you, for reading this far.

I meant this book to be non-fiction, but I've invented dialogue and have made assumptions. I've tried my best to make details accurate. All the mistakes are mine.